I'M DONE HERE!

I'm Done Here

Create Lasting Impact by Leading With Intentionality

Jason P. Armstrong

Published by Game Changer Publishing

Paperback ISBN: 978-1-964811-96-3
Hardcover ISBN: 978-1-964811-97-0
Digital ISBN: 978-1-964811-98-7

www.GameChangerPublishing.com

DEDICATION

To my beloved wife, Selina—your love is my greatest blessing, and your unwavering support has been the anchor in my life. This book is a tribute to the countless ways you've enriched my world, filling it with love, laughter, and endless inspiration. Every word is a reflection of the life we share, a life that I cherish more than words can express.

To my wonderful son, Jaxon, and my incredible daughter, Jase—this book is for you. You both bring so much joy, curiosity, and wonder into my life, and watching you grow has been the greatest adventure of all. Jaxon, your determination and kindness inspire me every day. Jase, your creativity and boundless energy remind me of the beauty in every moment. May you both always chase your dreams with courage and never forget how deeply you are loved.

To my loving parents, William and Jeanette Armstrong, amazing family, and cherished friends—this book is for you. Your support, love, and encouragement have been the pillars of my life, guiding me through every challenge and celebrating each triumph. To my family, you all have been my constant source of strength and inspiration—your presence fills my heart with gratitude every single day. To my friends, who have shared in laughter, adventures, and countless memories—your companionship has been a gift that I treasure beyond measure.

To all the incredible people who have helped me along this journey—this book is for you. Whether you offered guidance, support, encouragement, or simply a listening ear, your contributions have made all the difference. Every step forward has been shaped by your kindness, wisdom, and generosity.

Thank you all for being part of this journey and for helping me become the person I am today. This book is a testament to the impact you've had on my life, and I dedicate it to you all with profound gratitude.

Read This First

Just to say thanks for buying and reading my book, I would like
to give you a free welcome call with me, no strings attached!

Scan the QR Code Here:

ACKNOWLEDGEMENTS

"Jason Armstrong is a nationally recognized law enforcement leader. Just five years after the death of Michael Brown, Jason led the embattled police department in Ferguson, Missouri, through ongoing racial unrest, a global pandemic, and the rise of the Black Lives Matter movement. I personally know Jason to be a man guided by deep faith, an unshakeable love for his family, and an unwavering belief that we can all make the world a better place. In his memoir, *"I'm Done Here!"* Jason candidly shares the lessons, challenges, and rewards that come from making intentional decisions. It is a must-read for anyone seeking a service-driven career or a public-facing leadership role."

– Ronnie Mabra, Atlanta Attorney/Former Georgia State Representative

"From the title to the last page, 'I'm Done Here!' reads like a conversation with a friend—a funny, knowledgeable, relatable friend. While he has certainly earned the title of Chief, you'll want to call him Jason after reading this, as you'll feel as if you know him. His stories entertain and inform, and the lessons serve as a profound reminder that we can learn at any age, provided we are open to it. Our firm works daily with leaders of large and small organizations, all of whom stand to benefit from Jason's vast experience, so generously shared in 'I'm Done Here!'"

– Julie Parker, President & CEO of Julie Parker Communications

"I first met Chief Jason Armstrong when he arrived in Ferguson, Missouri, to take on the monumental role of Chief of Police while I was serving as Superintendent of the Ferguson-Florissant School District. Both of us are rooted in North Carolina, where our shared commitment to community and purpose was forged. Jason's book, 'I'm Done Here!' is a testament to his unwavering belief in the power of intentional leadership and the path that God has laid out for each of us. As Jason reflects, 'Striving to do the right thing should always be at the forefront of making decisions because you have to live with the outcomes of those decisions.' This quote captures the essence of his approach to leadership—rooted in integrity, purpose, and a deep commitment to making a lasting impact. I am honored to call Jason not just a colleague but a brother, as we continue to support each other in the important work we are called to do."

– Dr. Joseph S. Davis, Superintendent,
Ferguson-Florissant School District

"I first met Jason Armstrong during his tenure as Chief of Police in Ferguson, Missouri. We visited at length, sharing our thoughts on community engagement and how police departments can 'bridge the gap.' Our visions aligned, and because of that, I became intrigued with Jason and his passion for the betterment of humanity. As I followed his journey, we ultimately became friends, and I discovered that his heart shines brighter than his badge. I also learned he is a devoted husband and father. Jason is the type of leader who sets the standard for young officers beginning their careers by displaying a code of ethics that will mold these subordinates into future leaders. Jason is a breath of fresh air to the communities he serves. These communities aren't just people to him; they are his family. He is passionate, energetic, fair, and honest. Even as a supervisor overseeing entire departments, Jason continues to spend time in the 'trenches,' leading by example. Jason Armstrong has left an impact on every community he's served, and his heart continues to shine brightly!"

– Officer Tommy Norman, North Little Rock, Arkansas

"*Chief Armstrong and his friends, the Americans, connected with the Dominicans! Having played 14 years in the NFL, I learned how good leadership is connected with winning. In this book, Chief reminds us that we all can make a difference in places we never thought we could in order to make things better.*"

– Aeneas Williams, Lead Pastor at The Spirit Church/
Pro Football Hall of Fame

"*Chief Jason Armstrong has a unique perspective on the inner-workings of leadership during a challenging time and place. In 'I'm Done Here!' that perspective pours onto the pages as he eloquently, but very practically tells his story, particularly as it relates to 'THE Ferguson.'*"

– Wesley Bell, Congressman-Elect Missouri District 1

I'm Done Here!

*Create Lasting Impact
by Leading With Intentionality*

Jason P. Armstrong

www.GameChangerPublishing.com

Table of Contents

INTRODUCTION

Hello, my name is Jason Armstrong, and I want to thank you for doing me the honor of cracking open my first book. If my strategy worked, you opened this book saying to yourself, "I'm Done Here!? What in the world is this book about?" Stick with it and you will learn what the title and me are all about. Writing this book has been an amazing journey of reflection and appreciation.

So, who is Jason Armstrong? I was born and spent the early years of my life in East Orange, New Jersey. While still in grade school, my parents decided to move back to their home state of North Carolina, and we landed in Fayetteville. North Carolina would be my home until I graduated from the best HBCU in the land, North Carolina Central University, with a bachelor's degree in criminal justice. Seeking life in a bigger city, I moved to Atlanta, Georgia, where I started my law enforcement career in a suburb of the city. I am a husband, a father to two amazing human beings, a son, a brother, a friend, a mentor, and a dreamer—and some would call me a visionary.

Starting my career as a police officer, I had no clue what was in store for me and the impact that I could have on the profession. I became a student of the profession—and not just to be good at what I was doing. I studied the profession to try to understand why things happened. The

1

more I studied, the more I believed that I was uniquely positioned to make a difference. I saw a void in my community, and I knew that I had what it took to fill that void. When opportunities arose, I worked my butt off to take advantage of them. While the average age of police chiefs is around 46,[1] it wasn't by accident that I first reached the chief's seat at the age of 38. At 39, I would be appointed to one of the most notable law enforcement jobs in the world: police chief in Ferguson, Missouri.

Many people asked me why I would sign up for such a difficult task, but I've always had the mindset: *If not me, then who?* I was young and had enough vigor and confidence in my ability to build community that I went into Ferguson thinking, *To hell with me being ready for Ferguson; is Ferguson ready for me!* After experiencing the most challenging years of my life there, I can humbly admit that the city was absolutely ready for me and kicked my butt in the process. Nevertheless, it was an amazing experience for me, both personally and professionally.

Accomplishing so much at such a young age is both rewarding and challenging. I believe sharing my story will help others navigate the demands and challenges of leadership, regardless of what profession they are in. I wrote this book because so many people have heard parts of my story and asked me when my book was coming out. People saw the value in me sharing my journey, and I finally got to a point where I felt confident enough to put my thoughts into words and organize those words in a way that people would benefit from reading them. This book is a tribute to people who recognized things in me that I didn't always recognize in myself.

---

[1] Police 1, "State Your Case: How Young Is Too Young to Be a Police Chief," https://www.police1.com/chiefs-sheriffs/articles/state-your-case-how-young-is-too-young-to-be-a-police-chief-OWEXwPNdrW7zkWD8/#:~:text=of%20the%20list.-,With%20supportive%20peers%2C%20an%20inquiring%20mind%2C%20and%20a%20mix%20of,years%2C%20that%20seems%20about%20right.

While working on this book, I traveled to Orlando for a conference and met up with a friend of mine, Chris. He and I were talking over dinner about international travel, and I shared the story of an amazing experience I'd had while visiting the Dominican Republic several years earlier. I was there with a group of friends, and we opted to stay in the old city as opposed to a resort in the tourist area. Near our villa was a park, and walking by the park one day, we saw a huge crowd gathered to watch an intense game of pickup basketball.

The next day, my friends and I were down at the court, shooting around, when the "local team" showed up and challenged us to a game, Dominicans against Americans. Naturally, we accepted the offer, but we were severely outmatched. There were only six of us and about 15 of them. They were making substitutions, and they used players on their team as the referees. Understandably, we did not get any calls our way, and we lost the first game.

By the second game, we had adjusted to their style of play and the referee calls, and we won. By the third game, we were really locked in and clicking on all cylinders. Clearly, the word had spread that there was a big game going on at the park, and the crowd continued to grow and grow. By the third game, the park was packed. Kids were marveling at the shoes we were wearing (Kobes, Jordans, LeBrons), and people were set up on the bridge overlooking the park. It was something from a movie scene.

We ended up beating them pretty badly in the third game. Not wanting to be disrespectful on their home turf, we went to the bodega down the street and bought Gatorades for the opposing team as a sign of good sportsmanship—and also as a peace offering because we didn't want any problems with the locals during our stay.

After hearing that story, Chris told me that I had to share it in my book. He explained that the story highlighted what I brought to my law enforcement role as a bridge builder. I was out in the community, a different community at that, engaging with the people. I used something I was familiar with, basketball, as a tool to engage and connect with people. Although my friends and I ended up winning, it wasn't about winning; it was about the experience. We wanted to ensure we didn't disrespect the community since we were outsiders, and we were intentional about displaying respect for them and their community.

Chris said that this was exactly the kind of approach that he saw from me throughout our friendship. He highlighted that this story showed that community connecting was not just something that I did for work; it was part of the fabric of who I was. Thanks for the insight, Chris. That's why I wrote this book. I was simply sharing a fond travel memory, but through storytelling, we can accomplish so much more than just sharing memories; we can inspire the next wave of visionaries.

This book is for anyone who feels compelled to foster positive change. You do not have to be a law enforcement professional—heck, you don't even have to like the police to benefit from this book. The measure of your accomplishments is not always what you experience while you are in the leader's seat. The true measure of your success is how the organization is positioned for future success after you are gone. Whether you are already in a leadership position, aspiring to be a leader one day, or are just curious about what it takes to accomplish your wildest dreams, you will benefit from reading this book. If there's a community you want to impact positively, you are who I had in mind when I wrote this book.

Throughout my journey, I have wanted to show up for many communities. I wanted to show up for the law enforcement community. I wanted to show up for the community members I swore an oath to protect. I wanted to show up for the disenfranchised and marginalized members of the community, and I wanted to show up for the minority community.

Community has always been at the forefront of my success in law enforcement. I recognized the significance of building bridges with the community and how everyone would benefit if we did it the right way. The number one compliment I get from people is that I communicate with others with intentionality and genuineness. I don't see it as anything special; it's just me being me. But in the world in which I operate, clearly, it is a big deal.

I have earned several accolades throughout my career. I was awarded the 40 Under 40 award from my undergraduate alma mater, North Carolina Central University. I was awarded the Distinguished Alumnus in Public Service from my graduate alma mater, Columbus State University. I was awarded the 40 Under 40 award by the most notable law enforcement association in the world, the International Association of Chiefs of Police.

If none of that is impressive enough, I was selected for the inaugural USA Leaders program put on by former United States President Barack Obama's Foundation. Now, President Obama would not know me if I walked past him—he probably doesn't even remember my name. Knowing that he gave me a thumbs up when he could have given me a thumbs down is achievement enough for me.

Although I have gained a lot of noteworthy acclaim at the national level, community acclaim has meant the most to me. From local community organizations, I've received a Community Impact award, a Living Legends in the Community award, a Legacy award, and a host of certificates of appreciation. Showing up for the community has been my pride and joy, and the community has shown me their appreciation for doing so.

I hope that the pages ahead will be enlightening and entertaining and awaken a desire for you to be an agent of positive change—if that desire is not already burning inside you. I believe we all have the power to effect change; the challenge is to have the courage to manifest that power. Not everyone is comfortable leading. If leadership were for everyone, we wouldn't need leaders.

While writing this book, I received a text message from a former coworker. This was not someone I kept in regular contact with and our time together as coworkers did not grow into a friendship. The text message read, *"I want to tell you that I have really been reflecting on my career and although you and I did not always see eye to eye you made a huge impact in my life and career. I have watched you overcome adversity, excel, and do great things. You've never forgotten where you came from and you are an extraordinary leader. Keep trusting God and pursue all your goals. You've got this!! Have a great day."* That is what is beautiful about leadership. They may not see it at the moment, but hopefully people will grow to appreciate your contributions along the way.

After reading this book, you will be able to recognize opportunities in your life, whether personally or professionally, where you can have a greater impact. You will be bolder in seeing things through, and you will have greater confidence in your ability to overcome any challenge thrown at you.

I see too many people who lack the confidence to achieve the things that are truly meant for them. I can see it for them, but I can't make it happen for them. You have to create an environment where you thrive when opportunities arise or are on the horizon. I'm only successful because I set out to be successful. I wouldn't let anything stop me from achieving my goals. To understand how everything came to fruition, let's begin with how it all started.

CHAPTER 1

THE START

When I think about my time in law enforcement, I often go back to the beginning, when I didn't have a single thought about becoming a police officer. As a criminal justice major in college, I wanted to be an FBI agent or some other kind of federal agent. At the time, those were the law enforcement positions that got a lot of publicity and the cool TV shows. The only thing that gave me the slightest interest in a career in local law enforcement was the movie *Bad Boys*. I could see my younger self as a real-life Mike Lowrey (played by Will Smith), minus the wealth.

During my senior year in college, not many federal agencies were hiring individuals with no experience. That was when I started considering the idea of becoming a police officer for a short period of time, just to gain some experience, hoping it would make me more marketable to the FBI or another federal agency.

Around that same time, I learned of a program through the Department of Justice (DOJ) called the police corps. The appeal of this program was that the federal government would pay you up to $30,000 that you already spent obtaining your college degree. The program was a four-year commitment and you had to spend the entire four years working uniformed patrol, on the streets. The program was run at the state level, and the two states that I applied to were Maryland and Georgia. Georgia had more options as far as departments that were part of the program, so I focused on it.

My primary post-graduation goal was to leave North Carolina and move to a big city that had a lot going on, especially professional sports. I wanted to go to NBA and NFL games, and the Atlanta area offered me the ability to do that. After getting all my testing done, I was selected for the final interview board. The interview was on the morning of May 11, 2001. I remember that date because I was graduating from college the next day, and I had to hurry to get back to NC.

During my interview, I mentioned that I was graduating the next day. After my interview was complete and I was walking out of the room, one of the panel members, a black woman seated at the conference table, leaned away from the table, clearly trying to get my attention as I strode past. When I got close enough, she whispered to me, "Eagle Pride!" That was her way of communicating to me that she was an alumnus of North Carolina Central University. We both had big smiles on our faces after that exchange. I walked out of the room feeling very confident that I had at least one person on the panel who was going to vote for me to be accepted into the program.

A group of us were there to interview that day. Before we left, they told us if we had been accepted into the program. Fortunately, I made it in, and the flight back to North Carolina was much sweeter after learning that. Although it was not officially a job, it was a step in the right direction and worth celebrating along with my graduation. The Atlanta Police Department was not a part of the program, so I had to figure out which of the affiliated departments were close to the city. I remember getting on MapQuest and putting Atlanta as point A and then all the police departments in the program as point B to see which ones were closest. Forest Park bordered Atlanta, and it became one of my target departments.

As I mentioned, getting into the program did not equal getting a job, so I still had to apply and get hired by a department. I was excused from the program one day to go to Forest Park to turn in my application. The lady at the window who accepted my application told me that it had been a crazy morning and a plane had just crashed into a building in New York City. Turns out that the day I turned in my application to become a police officer was the darkest day in U.S. history for first responders and one of the darkest days in our country's history period. That day was September 11, 2001.

Being in the academy when 9/11 happened definitely impacted my view of the profession. Watching the footage from that horrific day really impressed upon me how dangerous the job was and how chaotic life could become in the blink of an eye.

As I progressed through the police corps, I completed the hiring process with Forest Park, so once I completed the program, I had a job waiting for me. The police corps wasn't too difficult. I learned a lot about doing the job, but more importantly, I learned about the complexities of professional life. One of the biggest lessons for me was the dynamic of race and understanding.

One morning, my police corps classmates and I piled onto the bleachers in the gym as we did every morning. The lead instructor, a white male, walked in with the rest of the instructor team and dropped a bomb on us. He started by saying, "Someone in here is a racist!" He went on to say that one of us had been reported to have used the N-word.

We were all shocked by this. At that time, there were four black males in the class; everyone else was a white male or female. The lead instructor asked for the culprit to stand. Everyone looked around, waiting for the culprit to identify themselves. When no one stood, the instructor continued to talk about the culprit and their actions. As he spoke, he stared at the classmate sitting right next to me. My classmate stood and said, "You must be talking about me since you're looking at me, but I'm not a racist!"

The instructor told my classmate to go to the office to await a private meeting. What was unique about how this played out is that it was one of the black males who was called out for being racist. Turns out that the four of us had been in the food line in the cafeteria, having a conversation, and my classmate had used the N-word as part of the regular conversation among us. It was not used in a derogatory way, but the person who overheard our conversation, another black person, had not appreciated it being said, regardless of the context, and reported it to our instructor.

This incident was a great lesson for me because it gave me insight into being a professional. I could no longer do all the things I had been doing in life. I had to mature and learn how to navigate life beyond my normal outlook. It also highlighted for me the challenge of leaders having to dissect someone's actions when there is a distinct cultural difference between the people involved. Although we were young, we understood the sensitivity of the N-word and how it was inappropriate in certain settings. At the same time, it was a part of our regular vernacular from childhood and not used in a negative way when we were talking amongst friends and peers.

> *This incident... highlighted for me the challenge of leaders having to dissect someone's actions when there is a distinct cultural difference between the people involved.*

I always had a problem with how the interaction kicked off that morning: "Someone in here is a racist!" That could not be further from the truth, and I felt there was a better way it could have been handled. At the same time, I recognize that it was probably the first time our instructor had needed to navigate a situation like that. This experience would come full circle for me years later when I was the person in the leadership role, and that word was uttered in a room full of people. I'll explain that situation a little later in the book.

Another lesson for me at the academy was getting one's attention to get results. One of the misnomers about law enforcement is that it is exciting and pulse-pounding all the time. That is not the case; the bulk of your time is spent talking to people and collecting information, and it is not very exciting. So, if parts of the job are relatively boring, sitting in a classroom and learning about them is even worse. It was a struggle to stay awake in some of our classes. That struggle is magnified if you have an instructor with no zeal or enthusiasm.

One instructor realized that my tablemate and I were not giving our undivided attention in his class, and he had just the right solution to change that. It was either after lunch or after a bathroom break, and the instructor was going through his monotone cadence, which was putting us all to sleep. The classroom had six-foot tables, so two of us sat at each. My tablemate, "W," was sitting on the left side of the table, and I was on the right. Our table was at the front of the classroom, closest to the door. W was turned in his seat, facing me, reading something that could have been a magazine—like I said, we were not paying attention to the instructor.

I heard a thud on the floor between W and me. At first, I thought W had dropped something. When I looked down to see what had hit the floor, I found myself peering at an object I hadn't seen before. It was metal, about six inches long, with metal caps on both ends, wires coming out of it, and nails wrapped around it. W and I must have reached the same conclusion at the same time because we both jumped up without saying a word and ran out of the classroom.

The instructor realized what had happened and ran out after us to keep us from running out of the building. The device was a replica pipe bomb used for training; it wasn't dangerous. The instructor had taped it underneath our table during the break, but the tape had given away, and it had fallen. The instructor explained that we were going to do a search exercise to look for the bomb later in the day. To this day, I'm still convinced that he chose our table because of our lack of attention in his class.

Our classmates were mad at us for not warning them of the danger before running out of the room. W and I were the two biggest people in our group, both college athletes, and our explanation was simple: "As big as we are, if you see us running, you don't need an explanation. Just know that you need to be running, too!"

I got through the five-month academy without any major hiccups and I was ready to officially begin my career. The early years were difficult because I was still young and immature, and I made a decent number of poor decisions. Luckily, my bad decisions did not cost me my job, as the department saw potential in me and just had to work with me to get me over the "nonsense" hump in my early days. These early challenges, along with the mercy and grace that were bestowed upon me, have become a great guide for me as a leader.

When I think about the start of my career and those early years, two situations stand out as the most impactful on my growth in the profession. These are very different from one another and can best be summed up as one highlight and one lowlight.

One question that I'm often asked is: "What has been your greatest accomplishment in your career?" The story that I always share is my interaction with a young man during a traffic stop that I made early in my career. At that time, I wasn't a supervisor; I was a line-level officer. What was significant about the Forest Park Police Department, and I'll speak more in-depth about this later in the book, is that we were very big on traffic enforcement.

Police departments across the country have different approaches to addressing challenges in the community. At that time, traffic enforcement was a primary focus for us in Forest Park. There is a natural correlation between tickets and arrests, as traffic stops drive those numbers. At the end of each month, the stats would get posted in the roll call (team briefing) room to show where everyone was in terms of ticket numbers. Unfortunately, some people in the department believed that making a lot of stops and writing many tickets made you a good officer, but in my opinion, that was an inaccurate correlation.

I was on patrol one night, operating a radar device, and I stopped a car for speeding. I approached the car and saw that the driver was a black male in his late teens or early twenties. When I checked his name in the computer system, it showed that he had an arrest warrant out for him. Once the backup officer arrived, I got the young man out of the car and put him in handcuffs while I waited for dispatch to confirm that the warrant was valid.

The young man couldn't believe that he had a warrant out for his arrest and was adamant that it must be some type of mistake. This is normal behavior; most people would be surprised to learn that they had a warrant. The warrant was confirmed through dispatch, and I informed the young man that he was going to jail.

For those who are not familiar with law enforcement, our computer system is the holy grail of information. If something is confirmed in the system, then it is a done deal from that point on. The young man continued to say that this must be a mistake, and he asked what the warrant was for. Since it was from another jurisdiction, I had limited information, but I shared what I knew from the information on my computer terminal. When I did, the young man told me that he had already been arrested for this offense. He asked me to call his mother, who could retrieve his jail and court paperwork to confirm he had already been to jail for this.

One thing that was extremely critical in this situation was the fact that the young man was being very respectful in how he spoke to me. Although upset, he was not lashing out, cursing, or insulting me for doing my job. I always try to go out of my way to be respectful toward people, and I always appreciate when the respect is reciprocated.

I called his mother and explained what was going on, and she, too, was adamant that there had been a mistake. She retrieved his paperwork and read the information to me. Two things immediately stood out to me from the information she provided: The date on the paperwork was after the date the warrant was issued, and the reference number she provided was the same number showing in the computer system. After speaking with the mother, I felt pretty confident that they were telling the truth and that the young man had already been to jail for this warrant.

This was my first experience with something like this, so I called the captain and apprised him of the situation. He asked me if the warrant had been properly confirmed through dispatch, which it had, and then he told me that there was nothing else to discuss and to take the young man to jail.

The captain had given me a direct order, so I followed it. However, he did not tell me how fast I had to drive to the jail or what phone calls I could make en route, so I had some flexibility there. I drove at a snail's pace while I made phone calls, trying to get someone on the phone who could confirm my belief that this young man had already been to jail for this offense. The challenge was that not only was it after hours, but it was a Friday night; there was no guarantee that anyone was going to call us back anytime soon. Dispatchers were assisting me with calling the after-hour numbers and trying to get a hold of someone who could provide additional detail about the status of the arrest warrant.

As I inched closer and closer to the jail, my fear of running out of time was starting to become a reality. By this point, I was pretty certain that this young man was not supposed to be going to jail, but I had little hope that I would be able to keep him out of jail that night.

When I turned into the jail parking lot, I heard my call sign come over the radio. Dispatch was asking me to call them immediately. I called them, and they explained that they'd finally gotten in touch with someone from the probation office who had confirmed that the warrant was not valid. I immediately pulled over and called the young man's mother to come pick him up.

While we were waiting, the young man and I had the chance to talk about life and the decisions we make. He really appreciated the fact that I'd given him a chance and listened to what he had to say. When his mother arrived, she gave me the biggest hug. I have never forgotten that hug. It made me feel amazing, and I was proud of myself for going the extra mile to help the young man. They left together, and I headed back to work. When I got back to the city, I explained to the captain that the warrant had turned out to be invalid, but the news was pretty much brushed off with a shoulder shrug.

While that experience is not that noteworthy compared to many heroic feats, what makes it so significant for me is the culture of my organization at that time. Raking up stats and numbers was often the focus, and I'd intentionally gone overboard to keep myself from getting some. I could be wrong, but I don't think many people in my organization would have gone to those lengths to keep that young man out of jail that night. Not because they were bad people—that just wasn't the culture of our organization. Once the captain made a decision, that was normally the end of it. I was proud of myself for not settling for that and going the extra mile to do the right thing. Although that was almost 20 years ago, it still stands out as one of my professional highlights.

Now, with the good comes the bad, and I had my fair share of "lowlight" situations in the early years of my career. When I speak with younger officers or young people in general, I often give this example of what not to do. I was working the night shift one evening. I had made my mind up before I got to work that I wasn't going to do any work that night. It was a Thursday night. I was a patrol officer, and this was in the second year of my career. I was working from 7:00 p.m. to 7:00 a.m., and I had a flight to catch Friday morning after work. I was traveling to New York City for a weekend to hang out with my best friend, Mike.

Going to work that evening, my only objective was to leave on time and avoid anything that would get me caught up there. I had to avoid reports, and the best way for an officer to do that was to be a backup officer for other officers. I was an all-pro backup officer that night. No matter where I was in the city, anytime someone needed a backup officer, I quickly jumped on the radio to get assigned.

The night was going great, and my plan was working to perfection. I'd gotten past the busy time, and I could see the finish line. Around 3:00 a.m., one of my colleagues made a traffic stop and asked for a backup officer, so I jumped all over it. The stop location was at one of the few 24-hour establishments we had in town, a BP gas station. When I arrived, my colleague explained to me that she believed the driver was not being truthful about his identity. In addition to the driver, there was another male and a female seated in the back seat of the vehicle.

As the investigation unfolded, the driver was removed from the vehicle, detained in handcuffs, and placed in the backseat of my colleague's patrol car. The male in the backseat was also eventually removed from the vehicle, put in handcuffs, and placed in the backseat of my vehicle. I remember my back window being cracked so I could communicate with the male. The female was also removed from the car, but she was not detained in handcuffs; she was standing with the lieutenant, who showed up shortly after I arrived.

My colleague asked me to assist her with searching the car. As I searched the back seat where the male had been sitting, I located a loaded gun and some drugs packaged for sale. Right then, I heard a noise that turned my attention back to where my patrol vehicle was parked. A wave of disbelief washed over me as I watched my patrol car make a U-turn and leave the parking lot.

I stood there, frozen, not knowing what to do. Then, I looked over at my lieutenant's patrol car and decided to go after my car. Leaping into action, I sprinted to the patrol car and opened the door. I paused to think about what I was doing. I told myself that I was in enough trouble already; taking the lieutenant's car was probably not a good idea. The lieutenant ran over, jumped in his car, and took off after my stolen patrol vehicle. Fortunately, there were two Clayton County Police officers in the parking lot—remember, this was one of the few 24-hour spots around—and the other officers took off after my car as well.

What ensued was a massive car chase that ended with the suspect driving into oncoming traffic on the wrong side of the interstate and ultimately crashing into the median divider to bring the pursuit to an end. I was picked up from the BP by my captain, and he drove me out to the crash scene on the interstate. Dozens of police cars were there.

By this time, I was dejected and feeling sorry for myself because I knew I was in big trouble for allowing this to happen. My patrol car was brand new, and the worst part about getting a new vehicle was being responsible for anything that happened to it. I sat on the median wall, and all the officers and state troopers involved in the chase walked by and asked if it was my car that had been stolen. Everyone was laughing and having a good time, thankful that they were not in my position.

We later learned that the suspect was able to maneuver the handcuffs under his legs and bring them to the front of his body. As far as getting into the driver's seat, there are only two possible explanations. It's possible the window was open on the cage divider separating the front seat from the back seat, but I don't think he was small enough to fit through it. The only other possibility is that he was able to stick his hands far enough out of the door window to open the door using the exterior handle. Personally, I believe he opened the door that way, and the noise I heard that caught my attention was the door closing as he got into the driver's seat.

Ultimately, I was written up for failure to supervise a detainee. I was held over at the end of the shift so the chief could be briefed on everything that had happened. Despite all of that, I still made it to the airport on time for my flight.

These two examples were great lessons for me early on in my career and definitely helped me mature. The first example taught me that we should always strive to do the right thing. Regardless of who has authority over you, you control how you show up in situations. Striving to do the right thing should always be at the forefront of making decisions because you have to live with the outcomes of those decisions.

As for the second example, the main takeaway is that shortcuts do not benefit you in the long run. When I'm talking to young people about the importance of professionalism, I hope that my ignorance and immaturity are things that they can benefit from. I use that story to push home the importance of having integrity and commitment to what you're doing on a daily basis.

Striving to do the right thing should always be at the forefront of making decisions because you have to live with the outcomes of those decisions.

Getting started in any career is hard. Maybe you are young, haven't experienced a great deal in life, and don't know how things will turn out. Maybe you are older and are concerned that you are starting a new career later in life. No matter what circumstance you find yourself in, the primary contributor to your success is how you show up. In my highlight scenario with the young man at the traffic stop, I had many barriers in front of me, but I was committed to helping until I exhausted every option. In my "lowlight" scenario of me not wanting to do any work that evening, I was my own barrier to my success that evening.

None of us start out with all the knowledge we need, but we can all start out with a high level of intentionality. I never could have imagined that my start would lead me on a magical rollercoaster ride that would take me to the highest heights.

CHAPTER 2

THE CLIMB

When I got to Forest Park, although the community was very diverse, the department was not. Everybody in the organization welcomed me, but several of the veteran black officers made it a point to connect with me and give me nuggets of advice early on. They were definitely a community within the police department.

One thing that stood out was that there was only one black supervisor in the entire department. He was a sergeant, the first level of supervision, but he was a school resource officer, so he didn't supervise anybody. As I learned more about the department, I discovered that sergeant was the highest level of supervision that a black person had achieved in the organization's history.

In my early years, when a promotion list would come out after the assessment process had concluded, the black officers would often finish at or near the bottom. I remember the rejection on their faces and the comments they would make that spoke to a feeling of hopelessness that blacks would never climb the ranks in the department. It wasn't just the black officers who worked at the department who were dismayed by the lack of diversity in supervision; some members of the community were just as concerned or frustrated by the lack of representation.

After working in patrol for a little over three years, I was recruited to our specialized unit, the V.I.P.E.R. (Variable Intense Patrol & Emergency Response) Unit. I was doing pretty well at that stage of my career, and people were starting to take notice.

One day, when some of my V.I.P.E.R. teammates and I were leaving a restaurant for lunch, a gentleman stopped me as I was passing his table. He asked if I was "Armstrong" and introduced himself to me. I knew who he was, although I had never met him before. I was familiar with him because he had run for mayor of Forest Park. "Mr. M" was his name. If he had been elected mayor, he would have been the first black mayor in the city's history.

My teammates had gone on to pay at the cash register, so it was just me standing there speaking with him. He explained to me that he was part of a group of community members who wanted to see diversity among leadership in the police department. He told me that my name had come up in this group as the best potential officer to ascend the ranks and reach the command level (captain or higher). He told me that his group would be putting pressure on the city's government and police leadership to make this a priority. After giving me his card, he said that his group wanted to meet with me outside of Forest Park while I was off duty. I didn't say much; I just listened as he ran through all of this with me. Then, I ended the conversation and went on to catch up with my teammates.

I never called Mr. M or met with the group he told me about. Once I'd processed what he had said to me, I didn't think it would be in my best interest to accept outside help to accomplish my goals. First, I didn't want to have my accomplishments attached to anything but the effort I poured into the job every day. Second, I didn't see how this group would be able to influence decisions inside the police department. I think this group had good intentions; it just wasn't for me. Although I never called Mr. M, and it would be several years before I ran into him again, that conversation made me realize that it was time for me to start climbing the ranks.

My first obstacle in the leadership climb was attaining the sergeant rank. I did exceptionally well in the process and finished number one on the promotion list. That meant that when the next sergeant position became vacant, I would get promoted to that position. It didn't take long before a position came open, but there was a catch. I was being promoted to sergeant and would have all the duties and responsibilities as every other sergeant, but my official title was "Acting Sergeant." The sergeant position I was filling belonged to someone who was being deployed overseas with the military. His position had to be held until his return. If he returned before another sergeant position came open, then I would be moved back to a non-supervisor position.

For the first four or five months of my tenure as sergeant, I was "acting." Another sergeant position became available, so my sergeant position was converted from acting to permanent, and the next person promoted took the acting slot. I had been a sergeant, in total, for approximately 14 or 15 months when the department announced that a lieutenant promotion process was forthcoming. I was extremely excited about this opportunity because I felt very strongly that I was a top candidate for the position.

Looking across the landscape of the department at that time, I knew there were only a small handful of people who were eligible for or interested in the lieutenant position. One thing about climbing the ranks inside a police department is that, most often, a promotion lands you in the patrol division if you are not there already. Many people decline to participate in these promotion processes because they have no desire to leave their current division, especially if it is a coveted assignment with an administrative schedule, Monday through Friday.

The operation's major facilitated promotional processes. When the eligibility list for lieutenant was posted, I was shocked to see that my name was not on the list. I knew I was eligible, so my first thought was that this was a simple error that needed to be brought to the major's attention. I went to the major's office to inform him of the error, and he told me that it was not an error. The conversation that ensued definitely fueled my passion to not only climb the ranks but do it my way and be authentically me throughout the journey.

When I asked the major why I wasn't eligible for lieutenant, he told me that the policy stated that you had to be a sergeant for one year first. I told him that I had been a sergeant for over 14 months, but he said that my time as "acting" did not count toward my time as a sergeant. This lame excuse made me furious. There is zero difference in what an acting sergeant and a permanent sergeant do.

The first thoughts that ran through my head were the sentiments of the black officers during my early years. Was this what they'd been talking about? Was I being denied because the department was not ready or comfortable to have someone like me at that level of the organization? To this day, I do not know if that had anything to do with the decision; I just felt that it was unjust. Of the list of potential candidates, I felt I was the strongest candidate in the group. My unconfirmed feelings at the time were that they wanted someone else over me but knew I would probably come in at the top of the list, so this was an easy way to keep me on the sidelines. I was happy for the person who got promoted to lieutenant, but it was difficult to watch because I felt I was the stronger candidate.

By the time the next lieutenant promotion process was announced, I had moved around a decent amount in the department. My first transfer was back to the V.I.P.E.R. Unit as the sergeant of the team. After a couple of years doing that, I was transferred to administration as the training coordinator for the department. That was the position I was in when the eligibility list came out for the upcoming lieutenant process.

At this point, I had been in the department for almost ten years. Sergeant was still the highest level a black person had achieved within the organization. The operations major was still the person who ran the promotion processes. In my current assignment as training coordinator, I reported to the administration major. Since I had been robbed of the opportunity to test for lieutenant the last time, I was very familiar with the process and what was supposed to happen this time around. Additionally, I knew who was eligible and potentially my competition for the position. However, when the eligibility list was emailed out, I was hit with another gut punch from the organization.

I was in my office when I opened the email and saw the list of names on the eligibility list. Several should not have been there according to our policy. My immediate response was, "Someone owes me an explanation!" I stormed out of my office and stopped outside the door of the administration major. I wanted to respect the chain of command and speak with him first. He was already speaking with someone in his office, and their conversation did not appear to be ending anytime soon. I paced outside his office for a while, but finally, I couldn't take it any longer. Leaving the administration wing of the building, I headed to the operations wing to speak with the operations major.

Storming into his office, I asked him how all these extra names were on the eligibility list when they didn't meet the policy requirements. He explained to me that they had decided to change the policy to give several people a chance to be promoted since they had previous supervisor experience from other departments. Once again, I questioned the motive here because all these individuals were white. Was this what the black officers were talking about when they would say that a black person wouldn't get a fair chance to climb in this organization?

"Why weren't these types of expectations explored years earlier when I was the one on the outside looking in?" I asked. He had no answer to that question. At this point, as a sergeant speaking to a major, I was out of line. I give the major credit because he understood my frustration, did not take it personally, and didn't pull the higher-rank card. However, I had one last thing to get off my chest, and then I would be done with my soapbox. I told the major not to misconstrue my frustration as a desire to avoid the competition of the process. I said to him, "I don't care who you put on that list. I'm going to bust everyone's ass there!" Then I strode out of his office. I might have said some stronger curse words than that, but my mom will read this book, and I don't want to get in trouble. (Hi, Mom!)

I held to my word. When the results were announced, I had finished first in the lieutenant testing process. There was a vacant position, so with that list announcement, I had just made history. I was going to be the first black lieutenant in the history of the Forest Park Police Department. I can't explain how proud of myself I was for that accomplishment. I had set a goal to break that glass ceiling, and I had done it. But I knew that I wasn't done yet, and I still had other accomplishments to tackle; this was just the beginning.

As you climb the leadership ladder, you get more responsibility, but you also start to get some flexibility in how you can handle matters and your people. I often revert to the "attention-getting" I noted earlier in my experience with the pipe bomb. As a leader, you have plenty of occasions when the people you lead are not paying attention, just as I wasn't in that academy class.

We had recently had a bank robbery, and my officers did not appropriately respond to the scene. We have policies that dictate the appropriate way to approach dangerous situations, and considering what's at stake in these matters, I wanted to make sure that my entire team knew what was expected and that they felt comfortable with how to respond to these types of calls.

During our shift briefing, I went over the policy with my team. As I looked out at them and saw their expressions and body language, I could tell that I was wasting oxygen. No one was paying any attention to what I was talking about. I finished the briefing on the policy, and then I asked the magical question: "Does anyone have any questions?" Naturally, I got none, which signified that everyone understood the policy and knew what to do the next time.

The next day, my team was stunned when I slapped them with a surprise pop quiz on the policy I'd covered the day before. I was disappointed by their lack of attention to the policy discussion; after brainstorming some attention-getting ideas, it was a pop quiz for the win. I told them that the results from the pop quiz were going into their personnel files. I was lying, but they didn't know that. Naturally, everyone failed the quiz. I received a lot of explanations and excuses as to why my surprise quiz wasn't fair, and the results should not go in their file. Needless to say, the next time I covered a policy during our briefing, I had a captive audience.

I'd been a lieutenant in the patrol division for about ten months when I was called to the office one day and informed that my captain had left, and we didn't know if she would be coming back. Well, the captain never came back, and from that day forward, I was the leader of our patrol shift. After several months, I was appointed acting captain, and I would serve in an acting capacity for a couple of years before I was eventually promoted to permanent captain, once again making history in my department.

One day, we were hosting a 5k run in Forest Park, and I was the captain on duty that day. I often went out to community events to engage with community members. That day, as I was walking through the crowd, I ran into a familiar face, Mr. M. This was the first time I'd seen him in person since our conversation in the restaurant several years earlier. Not only had we not seen each other in a long time, but he did not know that I had been promoted to captain. When Mr. M spoke to me in the restaurant that day, one of his comments was that his group wanted to see minorities at the command level. Now, there I was, standing in front of him, a member of the command staff. I can still see his eyes tracing all of the parts of my uniform and the smile on his face. His expression of pride at my achievement said it all.

At that moment, what resonated with me was that my accomplishments were much more than just mine. Mr. M saw them as his accomplishments, too. I don't know how long Mr. M had been fighting those battles. I don't know how long Mr. M had been trying to advocate for change. I don't know how long Mr. M had been advocating for representation and diversity for minorities in the police department. I don't know if he was also advocating in other Forest Park departments as well. But the interaction that we had that day really stands out as a pivotal moment for me in my career.

Until that point, I was selfish in how I looked at things. What I had accomplished was all about me, and I didn't think about its significance to others. How did my fellow minority officers feel about it after all they had been through? Whether the challenges were perceived or reality, their feelings were real. How did the community feel about seeing representation at that level for the first time? Standing in front of Mr. M that day was a humbling experience because he saw something that I don't think he thought he would see in his lifetime. For me, that spoke to the power of what my accomplishments represented and the responsibility that I carried to ensure that I was not the last to achieve those heights.

One thing that I regularly do throughout my daily life is run scenarios through my head of all the things that could go wrong wherever I may be at the time. I started doing this as a young officer as I rode around on patrol, thinking of the craziest things that could unfold in front of me and how I would react to them. In running those scenarios through my head, I always survived whatever crazy situation my creative brain could conjure up. I never really thought about bad things happening to me as a police officer because I constantly told myself that I could handle any situation and would survive any encounter. Once I became a supervisor, however, fear crept into my head—the fear that something bad might happen to one of my officers. On November 8, 2017, my fears came to reality.

One thing that I regularly do throughout my daily life is run scenarios through my head of all the things that could go wrong wherever I may be at the time.

I was attending a training class, so I was not working my regular schedule or working directly with my team. I was slated for class Monday to Friday that week, but my team was only working Wednesday and Thursday of that week. The training was at an off-site location on the outskirts of the city. That Wednesday, while I was sitting in class, one of my coworkers jumped up with his phone in hand and shouted, "Two of our officers just got shot!" I immediately asked him who had been shot because my patrol team was on duty at that time. That meant two of *my* officers had just been shot. He couldn't tell me who it was, but we ran out of the training room, jumped into the major's vehicle, and rushed to the scene.

When we arrived, I jumped out and saw all of my officers were there, including my lieutenant, who was second-in-command on the team. I ran up to him and asked, "Who is it, and what happened?" He told me which two officers had been shot, one in the leg and one in the neck. I remember it like it was yesterday when the lieutenant told me about the officer who was shot in the neck. My lieutenant said, "It's bad!" and that was all he kept saying: "It's bad. It's bad." He motioned with his hands to show me how the officer had been holding his neck together when they'd arrived. He was still conscious and alert when they got there, so that was a good sign. Both officers had already been transported to the hospital by the time I arrived. We didn't know who the suspect was or where he had gone, so a perimeter was being set up, and more officers were arriving. We had put out the call that officers were down, and we had a manhunt underway for the shooter.

I had no equipment, no gun, no radio, no vest, and I wasn't in uniform. There were two higher-ranking officials on the scene already, so I was confident that the scene had what was needed regarding leadership. My immediate thought was, *I need to get to the hospital ASAP.* My biggest fear was that my officer was going to die alone, surrounded by strangers. I just wanted to get to the hospital in hopes of getting to him before he died. I explained to "Major T" with the fire department that I needed to get to the hospital, and he told me to jump into his fire command vehicle, and then he whisked me off to the hospital.

I remember thinking on the ride, *This is going to hit the news real soon, and the only thing that they're going to know is that some officers in Forest Park have been shot.* I decided to call my wife and tell her what was going on. Up until this point, I'd been fine, responding automatically to events as they unfolded. But when I heard my wife's voice on the phone, all my bottled-up emotions came pouring out, and I started crying uncontrollably. I cried so hard that I couldn't get any words out. She started crying, too, because, clearly, something was catastrophically wrong, but she didn't know what it was because I couldn't get the words out. With the help of Major T, I was able to pull myself together and finally tell her what had happened. I asked her to make phone calls and post on social media to let everyone know I was okay.

We got to the hospital, and I made my way to the room where they were preparing the officer to go into surgery. He was still conscious and alert when they rolled him out. As he rolled past me, I was able to talk to him for a second. I don't remember what I said to him, but I do recall that he told me who on our team to talk to because they would know who to call. I mustered up some words of encouragement and support, but honestly, I never thought I would see him alive again.

As the hours went by, people piled into the waiting room with me to wait for the update. When it came, it was the best news possible. He was out of surgery and still alive. He was not out of the woods yet, but he was still with us. After hearing that, I went over to the other hospital to check on my other officer. He was doing fine, all things considered, and was soon to be released from the hospital. Feeling much better, I got a ride back to the station, where my team was waiting for me to return with an update. I briefed them on the status of both officers, and everyone was released to leave.

While at the hospital, I'd learned that they had located the suspect. It turned out that my officers had fired their weapons once the suspect started firing at them, and he had been struck. The suspect had been able to run away and hide, but by the time he was located, he had died from his wounds. By the grace of God, both officers would survive their injuries. The officer shot in the leg was able to return to full duty. After a long recovery, the officer shot in the neck was able to return to work in a limited role, but he was never able to be an officer out on patrol again.

My officers being shot really took a toll on my emotional health. What few people knew at the time was that my aunt had just passed away the weekend before the shooting. I still remember how, when I arrived home the evening of the shooting, seeing my family brought tears to my eyes. I can't explain what I was feeling; I was just extremely emotional.

A few days later, a group text message came out to my team about scheduling a meeting with the psychologist. The message instructed everyone to reply individually with the time slot they wished to get for their meeting to maintain the anonymity of the process. Unfortunately, the meeting was voluntary, so I was worried that a lot of my folks were going to opt out. I scheduled my meeting for the first available time slot, and then I shared that with the team. I went on to tell them that it was okay to not be okay. We had been through a traumatic experience, and we needed to accept the help that was available to us. I knew I was having a hard time with my emotions, but I also knew that I was not alone.

I made my ploy to the team, and then I left it alone. I don't know who met with the psychologist after I did, but I found the session very helpful. The psychologist helped me understand why my family was so triggering for my emotions.

What helped me the most was attending a church service that weekend. We had traveled to Fayetteville, NC, for my aunt's funeral. Fayetteville is most famous for being home to Ft. Bragg (now Ft. Liberty) and the 82nd Airborne Division. There was a special guest speaker that day in church, a colonel from the Army. During his speech, he shared about an attack his platoon suffered while out on a mission. It just so happened that one of his soldiers was in the audience that day. I can't remember if any soldiers were killed in that attack, but some were definitely hurt.

I speak openly about the trauma that we experience in this career because we have a lot of men and women who are suffering in silence, and the profession's suicide numbers are proving that we are losing this battle.

As he shared this story, I played in my head what had just happened with my officers and my team. The colonel was not out in the field with his platoon when they were attacked. He was speaking from the place of being the leader of people when tragedy strikes. He got emotional and started to cry. By now, I was full-on crying, too, but this time, I knew why. I was crying from a sense of relief that what I was experiencing was normal. This attack had happened many years earlier, but just talking about it drummed up intense emotion for the colonel. At that moment, I knew I would be okay. I just had to go through the process of dealing with what had happened. I speak openly about the trauma that we experience in this career because we have a lot of men and women who are suffering in silence, and the profession's suicide numbers are proving that we are losing this battle.

While the shooting was the most traumatic experience for me during my tenure with Forest Park, the most significant was something that I did not even experience directly. The aftermath of the shooting death of Michael Brown Jr. in Ferguson, Missouri, in August 2014 was unlike anything I had witnessed during my tenure in law enforcement. The rioting, looting, and burning buildings all seemed unreal as they played out daily on the news. I was very intrigued by what was happening there, and I followed the story more than I had any other news story before.

The following year, the Department of Justice released its report on the Ferguson Police Department, and I read it. That report changed my career and, essentially, my life. I was blown away by the similarities between how community members were talking about the Ferguson Police Department and how some community members talked about us in Forest Park. If that same shooting had happened in Forest Park, would we have seen a similar response from people in the community? One thing I knew for certain was that I didn't want to find out.

I was still the only minority in the command staff. The community was overwhelmingly minority by this time, and I felt I was uniquely positioned to lead the charge of community bridge-building. The primary ingredient in my commitment was intentionality. Later in the book, I will dive deeper into the nuts and bolts of the work that lay ahead for me, but the significance of this moment on my climb to the top can not be understated. This was the moment when I started to come into my own as a leader. I now understood why Mr. M was advocating for diversity in leadership.

Once I started to be more intentional about bringing more awareness to my department about why some people felt the way they did about the police and what we could do to help change their outlook, I really started to find my voice in the department. The work didn't require heavy lifting from people; we just needed to be more mindful about how we showed up for the community—for everyone in the community. I felt very strongly that this was what we needed from the department for us to get better, but I would learn that not everyone was ready to tackle the internal change that we needed to undergo as an organization.

I attended a department training session one evening on community policing. I was looking forward to this because I was eager to see what new strategies and information the department was going to share that would contribute to us being more intentional about how we showed up and engaged with the community. The class was being taught by the department's training coordinator, who was a sergeant. It didn't take long for me to realize that this class was the same watered-down community policing overview class that did nothing to challenge officers to be intentional about how they engaged with the community.

An opportunity arose in the class for me to explain my thoughts on why we were not reaching our full potential as an organization and were so disliked by segments of the community. I spoke very directly about our emphasis on tickets and how that led to us not building the relationships we needed. Once I got on my soapbox, I kind of took over the class.

Although I was the only black person in the room, many of the other officers agreed with what I was talking about.

Clearly, the training coordinator did not appreciate the direction the class went after I got involved, and my comments landed me in the chief's office the next day. Before being summoned, I was put through the wringer by my major because the chief had scolded him for having an insubordinate captain. Once the major gave me a chance to explain everything, he was not as mad as when the conversation first started. He understood where I was coming from. He instructed me to write a statement explaining my side of things because the training coordinator had already produced a statement on his.

What neither I nor the major knew was that the chief was not done with his rants, and after the major left for the day, I was called down to the chief's office. The chief went on to chew me out for what the training coordinator had reported about my comments, even accusing me of being politically motivated. Every time the chief asked me a question, and I began to answer, he would cut me off and go back to chewing me out. I never got an opportunity to explain my side of things.

I have to admit that this experience hurt me. I would have been okay if the chief hadn't liked what I had to say, but the fact that he took one side of the story and made up his mind about what had happened really hurt. What also hurt was that I was a captain, and my accuser was a sergeant, and I didn't get any respect as a commander before being judged. I had no intention to disrespect the sergeant or the training, I just felt compelled to speak up. The sergeant was well within his right to voice his displeasure with me in the training, but I felt I should have been afforded the opportunity to explain before being chastised. I was able to provide a written statement, and leadership spoke to some of the other people who were in the room for the training and got a differing perspective on what had transpired and what I'd said. I had not bad-mouthed the department; I'd only spoken from my direct experience.

The following week, I had a follow-up meeting with the chief, and his tone was completely different. He was now asking me to assist with facilitating the training class in the future. While his demeanor suggested he realized he'd been premature in his handling of the information he'd initially received, he never apologized for treating me that way. That experience definitely shaped my outlook on the department and the chief, and I didn't see myself remaining with the department for much longer.

Soon after, I started applying for chief jobs in the metro Atlanta area. I felt confident in my abilities to lead. After months of rejection letters and emails, I still remember the day I checked my home mailbox and found a letter from a city I had applied to for the chief's position. At first, it had the same canned language that all my other rejection letters did, but then it took a turn for the good. Instead of saying, "We regret to inform you," this letter said, "We would like to congratulate you."

I was elated to have the opportunity to interview for a chief position. I had done all the things to position myself to compete for one of these jobs. I had obtained my master's degree, completed Georgia's Law Enforcement Command College, and participated in Georgia State University's International Law Enforcement Exchange Program; these were all the things that seemed to be what you needed to be competitive for a chief job in Georgia.

After my interview, I was convinced that I had done well and made a good impression on the city manager and council members. Ultimately, though, I was beaten out by one of my command college cohorts, but I was happy for him. I still have that interview letter to this day. It was a great experience, and I gained invaluable insight into the chief interview process.

Right after that, another position in the area opened up. I was selected to interview for that one as well, and I made it through a couple of rounds before I was nixed from consideration. I was feeling really good about where I was, and I was gaining more and more confidence that I had what it took to be a chief.

As fate would have it, rumors started to swirl around Forest Park that our chief might be leaving soon. Forest Park had just elected its first black mayor, and the majority of the council was also black at this point. A few of the council members were known to publicly speak out against the police department and the chief in particular. There had been some very high-profile incidents involving the previous mayor that had not shined a favorable light on the city. One in particular involved the police department.

As rumors intensified, news stories started to come out in the local papers that the chief was being forced out due to racial profiling practices within the police department. In addition to the rumors of the chief leaving, rumors were also swirling that I was going to be appointed the interim chief once he was gone. It was a crazy time in Forest Park, and things were extremely tense for the department and community. The situation was playing out very publicly, and that was not good for anyone.

On October 1, 2018, Forest Park's council meeting was jam-packed, standing room only. We all suspected that the council was going to decide on the chief at that meeting. Things had been boiling up too much in the community and the media; something had to be said or done to bring closure to the drama. By this point, from what I was hearing through unofficial sources and people who were reporting comments back to me, I believed I would be appointed the interim chief if the chief was let go.

Although I wanted to become chief, I was not at all happy with how everything was unfolding. The chief and I had our differences and disagreements, but he had dedicated over 40 years of service to the community, and I hated to see that end the way it was.

After some prepared statements by council members, they left the chambers for a closed session and returned a short time later. Upon their return, a motion was made to terminate the chief, and it passed with a three-to-two vote. Immediately following, another motion was made to appoint me the interim chief, and it also passed three to two. What was significant about the three-to-two vote was that it was all black council members on one side and all white on the other. With the now-former chief being white and me being black, this made the perfect storm for naysayers to conclude that I was only picked because I was black. One comment that made it back to me that was allegedly said by one of my fellow captains was that I had clearly sold my soul to the black council members.

After the meeting concluded, I was summoned to the back to speak with the city manager and city attorney. I ran into the chief back there as well, and he turned some items over to me. Clearly, it was an emotional moment for both of us. The only thing he said to me was, "Take care of my folks." I promised him I would.

I only served as interim chief for a few months. I was blindsided one day and informed that the council no longer wanted me to serve in that role, and I was going back to my captain position. When I asked the city manager why, her answer was, "All I can say is that you're caught up in politics." Little did I know, but the politics would get way worse. After being selected as a finalist for the permanent chief position, the council pressured the city manager to remove me from the process. Once again, no explanations were provided to me. My assessment of the situation is that a contingent of the council that didn't want me in the chief's seat was worried that I would be the top candidate in the process, which would make it harder for them to get the *handpicked* candidate some of them wanted.

That was the final straw for me in Forest Park. I knew I needed to leave before I told some people what I really thought about them and ended up getting fired.

My short stint as the interim chief was a whirlwind of an experience. I learned a great deal in that time, but most importantly, I learned that I still had a great deal to learn to successfully navigate the challenges of being a chief. I began a national search for opportunities that I thought were a good fit. One day, while on vacation, I got a call from a city that would change the trajectory of my career beyond my wildest imagination.

CHAPTER 3

THE FERGUSON

One day, while searching for chief jobs, I came across a familiar name: Ferguson. Ferguson, Missouri, was looking for a police chief. When I read through the job posting, two things stood out to me immediately. The first was that there was no way I was qualified or stood a chance of becoming the chief there. The second was that I was shocked to see that they were not asking for candidates to submit one of those 50-page applications. The only thing they were asking for was a cover letter and resume. I had both of those ready to go, so I thought, *Why not?* I sent off my package and didn't think anything else about it. It was really more of a joke to myself that I had applied to be the police chief in Ferguson.

Several weeks later, I got a call from the interim city manager, and he invited me to come to Ferguson to interview for the position. Despite this, I still did not think there was any chance I would be considered for the job. The day I arrived in Ferguson, there happened to be a council meeting that evening. After my complicated council experience in Forest Park, I was curious to see how this council acted and conducted business. Attending that meeting changed everything for me and my outlook on the interview process.

During the public comment portion of the meeting, a community member told the council that they needed to start over with the chief search because rumor had it that there were only two candidates left and that was not a quality applicant pool. I remember thinking to myself that this community member didn't know what they were talking about because I had seen the interview schedule and I knew that several of us were interviewing. The interim city manager told the audience that five candidates had been selected to interview, but over the weekend, three of them had pulled out. I'm sure my eyes bulged out of my head at that moment. That meant that it was just me and the internal candidate remaining in the process.

When I talked to my wife that evening, I told her that she needed to start processing the notion of us moving because I was about to be offered the job. It wasn't that I thought I was any better than the internal candidate; I just saw myself as different and more of what was needed to bring about change. The internal candidate had way more experience than I did and had been a chief for many years, but I saw this as my time to shine. Over the next two days, I went through three interviews each day, and I felt more and more confident after each one. By the time we had finished the process with a town hall-style Q&A event, I knew I had done it.

Although I was confident that I would be offered the job, my wife was reluctant to discuss the possibility of us moving because she was not mentally ready to face the idea of leaving Atlanta. The following week, the interim city manager called me and offered me the job. I told him I would have to talk it over with my wife and would call him the next day with an answer. My wife and I discussed it that evening, and it was clear to me that she was completely distraught over the idea of leaving Atlanta. However, at the end of our discussion, she told me that she supported me taking the job and us moving to Missouri.

The next morning, I called the interim city manager and turned down the job. He was caught off guard and befuddled at my decision. I explained to him that my wife was not where I needed her to be for me to take the job. After some back and forth, we ended the call, and I felt comfortable with my decision. I knew I was going to be in trouble because I didn't tell my wife I was going to turn down the job.

A few hours later, he called me back and asked if my wife was the real reason I was turning down the job. I explained that I understood how big of a challenge this would be and how taxing it would be to take this on. The only way I saw myself surviving this challenge was with my support system being able to carry me when I had nothing left to carry myself. If my wife weren't able to carry me when I needed it, my whole family would suffer, and I couldn't let that happen. He offered to bring the two of us up for a visit so my wife could see the area for herself.

> *The only way I saw myself surviving this challenge was with my support system being able to carry me when I had nothing left to carry myself.*

That evening, I talked with my wife and told her everything that had unfolded. She was mad at me for turning it down, but she understood where I was coming from. We went for a visit and, upon returning, did a lot of praying and consultation with trusted advisors and loved ones.

An unexpected source of guidance during that time came from former First Lady Michelle Obama. My wife went to see her on her book tour right in the middle of our wrestling with this decision. Mrs. Obama shared her reservations about her husband running for office. She had no interest in politics, but she believed in his vision and purpose. She also had peace with the understanding that his political journey was only going to be a season of their life, not the rest of it. That helped my wife see us moving to Ferguson in the same light and helped us with the decision to go.

You probably noticed that the "THE" in the title of this chapter was written in capital letters. That was intentional because of my experience whenever I tell someone I was the chief in Ferguson. When I mention Ferguson to people, I'm usually met with a familiar expression as they ask themselves, "Why do I know that name?" Then, when it clicks for them, a questioning look comes to their face, and they ask, "THE Ferguson?" It has become comical to me at this point, so I have personally dubbed Ferguson "THE Ferguson."

I could write an entire book just on the Ferguson experience, and one day, I probably will, but for now, I'll just hit on the highlights. I was the chief there for exactly two years. Over those two years, I had to contend with the fifth and sixth anniversaries of Michael Brown's death, the COVID pandemic, rioting, and civil unrest in the aftermath of George Floyd's murder, federal oversight, and a host of other community and department challenges.

I admit that I underestimated the significance of becoming the chief in Ferguson. I remember the night the council met to vote on my appointment as chief. My wife and I watched a livestream courtesy of The Real STL News—more on them later—and after I was confirmed, I thought I would wait until the morning to share the news on social media. Well, the news spread like wildfire, and my phone was buzzing like crazy. News articles were already coming out, and friends were tagging me in social media posts sharing the news. The following day, I got a call from a St. Louis-area reporter on my personal cell phone, and he refused to answer how he'd gotten my personal number. I had just stepped into the big leagues, and now it was my time to show I belonged.

My first challenge was the media frenzy; not only was Ferguson getting a new chief, but it was only a few weeks until the fifth anniversary of Michael Brown's death. Early on, I met with the Brown family, and they explained all the events they were planning. We worked with them to ensure we were on the same page with what was going on. I also met with a group of local activists and tried to have a dialogue with them about what protest events they had planned for the anniversary. They declined to share any of their plans with me, but they smirked at each other when I asked the question. Clearly, they had something planned, but they were not going to share anything with me.

The biggest part of our planning and preparation was done in conjunction with agencies that would provide aid if the situation escalated beyond our capacity to handle. Ferguson was a small city of around 22,000 residents, and we had less than 40 officers at that time. Relying on mutual aid from county police, the state highway patrol, and surrounding municipal agencies was the only way we could manage a large-scale incident.

On the day of the anniversary, the first event is always the memorial service. The service is held on Canfield Dr., where Michael Brown's body lay in the street after he had been shot and killed. I had only been in Ferguson for a few weeks, so I only knew a limited number of people in the community. I didn't know what to expect at the memorial service, but I wanted the community to see that I was present. Even if it meant being in an uncomfortable environment, I was going to show up.

I have to admit, once again, I underestimated the magnitude of Ferguson. When I attended the memorial service, I did not take any other officers with me; it was just me. Upon arrival and walking through the crowd, I immediately felt that I had made a mistake in coming down there. People were staring at me with hate and anger in their eyes, to the extent that I feared I might get attacked. The family knew I was going to be there, but no one else knew. I was in uniform, and I represented the source of their pain. I was a symbol of the reason Michael Brown was not alive.

Although it had been five years, the pain was still very raw, and I was a staunch reminder of that pain.

I made it through the service and left the area without any problems. Other community events followed the memorial service, and they all went off without any noteworthy issues.

That evening, I had just finished eating dinner at a nearby restaurant, and as I was walking back to the police department, I saw droves of cars pulling into the parking lot across the street. I immediately knew what was going on: a protest was about to kick off. Dozens of people strolled into the roadway, with a few of them holding a banner that said the road was going to be closed for the next four and half hours to commemorate the length of time Michael Brown's body lay in the street on the day he died. Who was holding the banner and leading the effort? Of course, it was the activist members I had met with earlier that week.

I got on the radio and notified my team that protestors had taken to the streets in front of the police department. In addition to the activists and protesters, media members and one of my council members were with the group. I tried multiple times to convince them to move the protest out of the roadway, but they refused. Finally, I gave the order for officers to move in and start making arrests. The leaders of the group remained in the roadway and were arrested; everyone else moved to the sidewalks.

For the next several hours, protestors crossed the roadway back and forth to disrupt traffic but not stop it. A few people hurled insults and slanderous banter at me and my officers. For digital readers, you can find photos from that evening's events here: X (formerly Twitter).

I never had to call in assistance that evening, though I have to admit, in the beginning, I was seriously considering making the call. I was nervous about how things were going to play out, and I didn't want to get it wrong. My reserve paid off, and the night was a success. We ended up deploying officers on both sides of the street to help the protestors cross back and forth. We had the same resources in place for the next evening, but no one showed up. The anniversary weekend was over, and we had handled everything as well as we could have.

For those who are not familiar, Ferguson is under a federal consent decree with the Department of Justice as a result of an investigation into the police department after the shooting death of Michael Brown. A consent decree is a court order of mandates that Ferguson must comply with. Consent decree objectives are worked on with the DOJ team, and once we agree on the objective, the matter is sent to the monitor for their approval.

In the months following the anniversary, I primarily dealt with the DOJ on our reform efforts. We had hired a new consent decree coordinator, Nicolle Barton, who was a civilian oversight practitioner. This was the first time since Ferguson's consent decree had been issued that the person responsible for compliance and implementation was not a sworn officer. Under the consent decree, we had a status hearing every three months with the federal judge the case was assigned to. At the last status hearing, before I started, the monitor had been very critical of the department for its lack of momentum in implementing reforms. In the first status hearing after I arrived, with the new consent decree coordinator in place, we received a decent report from the monitor and DOJ.

I'll go more in-depth about reform work a little later in the book, but we were making progress, and things were looking promising. We had made it through the anniversary without any setbacks. We had some new people in key places and were gaining momentum. I was getting more acclimated to the department and the community. I was starting to build relationships with people in the community and finding new partnerships to highlight that we were a different department from years earlier. However, in January 2020, a lot of that momentum came to a screeching halt, and that would be the beginning of the most stressful year of my life.

That month, I had my second status hearing. I had been in Ferguson for six months at that point. Every status hearing has a public portion where anybody can show up and make comments. Some people regularly showed up to complain about what we weren't doing or what they weren't seeing from the police department.

Since we typically received negative comments, the interim city manager had told me that he was going to speak during this part of the hearing, but he didn't tell me what he was going to talk about. He was the last person to speak that day, and boy, did he drop the mic. He highlighted three challenges the city was facing, with the consent decree being one of them. Each of the challenges had a financial burden attached to it, and he ended his comments by stating that if the city didn't successfully resolve these issues, we would need to seriously consider dissolution. Dissolve the city? No city meant no police department, and no police department meant no police chief. No police chief meant I had no job, and none of my staff had a job. I had uprooted my family to take this position, and six months in, I was slapped upside the head with this bombshell. To say I was furious is an understatement; I was livid!

The day after the status hearing, officers lined up outside the captain's office, asking for an explanation. Several officers asked if they needed to find another job because they didn't want to be blindsided by layoffs from the city dissolving. I went to talk to the interim city manager to see if he had a game plan to address the staff's concerns. He told me that his comments were not meant for staff but were a "shot across the bow" for the DOJ. I explained to him that despite his intentions, many staff members were seriously concerned about what he'd said. I tried to explain the severity of the moment and the impact his comments had on the department but he did not seem to comprehend the magnitude of the problem. I told him I had to figure out a way to calm the storm at the police department but that he needed to seriously consider putting a message out to all town staff because the police department was not the only city department impacted by his comments.

Since the interim city manager did not convey any intention of addressing his comments with the staff, I took it upon myself to email the police department. I acknowledged the impact of his comments and explained how they had affected me. I stated that I was not speaking as the chief; I was speaking as a husband and father who had just uprooted his family to take this job and was now faced with the same uncertainty that they were. Staffing was already at a critical level for us, and it was difficult to recruit people to come work in Ferguson. I needed them to understand that a city couldn't dissolve overnight and wasn't something that could be done secretly and with no notice. I promised to keep them informed if I ever caught wind of that being the direction the city was headed in, and I begged for their trust in the matter. Little did I know that this was just the beginning of the turmoil.

Shortly after the status hearing, life as we knew it would change as governments across the globe began implementing mandatory lockdowns in response to the spread of the coronavirus (COVID-19). No one was ready for how our lives were going to be impacted by COVID-19. It was especially difficult to be a first responder because there are no remote options to perform your job. We were able to send some administrative staff home to work, but for the most part, the bulk of our folks continued to come in to work most days. As administrators, we initially tried to do some remote work, but it didn't last long. We needed to be in the building, and people needed to see us making the same sacrifices that they had made.

Resources were scarce, especially N-95 masks, and the media reporting on COVID-19 made it seem that if you didn't have one, you were in serious trouble. Despite the lack of resources and the uncertainty that we all were experiencing, we handled the challenges pretty well. A fair share of staff members contracted the virus, but thankfully, we did not lose anyone to it. However, just as we were adjusting to the new norms of navigating life through a pandemic, the world would get dealt another huge blow.

On Memorial Day (May 25th), 2020, a video clip started circulating on social media. The video was of the arrest of George Floyd by the Minneapolis Police Department. We would soon learn that the video showed the death of George Floyd. It didn't take long before Minneapolis experienced significant civil unrest in the aftermath of George Floyd's death. Derek Chauvin was the Minneapolis police officer who held his knee on George Floyd's neck after he was already handcuffed. Chauvin was terminated immediately and under investigation for criminal charges, but none of that mattered. The unrest quickly intensified in Minneapolis and then spread to other cities across the country. Within a couple of days, local activists in Ferguson started calling for protests across from the police department in the afternoons. By the middle of the week, we saw advertisements for a big protest in Ferguson on Saturday, May 30.

On May 28, the situation reached its pinnacle in Minneapolis as rioters set fire to a police precinct headquarters building. As I watched the building burn on live television, it took me back to watching the destruction in Ferguson after Michael Brown was killed. Seeing how bad things had escalated in Minneapolis, I was extremely worried that we were going to see the worst of the worst at the big protest on Saturday.

The protest was scheduled for late afternoon. By this point, things were so crazy around the country that I didn't feel comfortable with my family staying at home while I was at the protest. My wife had scheduled a prayer call with our family and friends before I left home to face whatever was coming our way that day. Once it concluded, my family packed up and went to stay with friends so I didn't have to worry about people showing up at my home and harassing them.

Hundreds of people came out to protest that day. We had activated mutual aid, so I had a contingent of mobile field force officers on the property, but they were hidden. The plan was to only use Ferguson officers in regular uniforms to handle the crowd, and if things escalated beyond our control, we would activate mutual aid, and mobile field force teams would deploy from inside the building to engage with rioters. According to standard Incident Command System guidance, I was supposed to be set up at the command post, which was away from the police department where mutual aid response was being coordinated. With the magnitude of what we were dealing with and my fear of this protest escalating to unrest, I felt I needed to be on the ground and in the mix of things to have a handle on what decisions needed to be made at the moment.

Once protestors flowed into the police department parking lot, I was out there amongst the crowd. I planned to talk to as many people as I could and hoped they realized the police were just as disgusted by what we had seen in the video as they were. Not too many people cared to hear what I had to say; they were too busy yelling and screaming at me. I tried to explain to people how Ferguson was different after years of reform work since Michael Brown's death.

For several hours, protestors voiced their concerns and issues, and my officers and I listened and engaged in dialogue with many of them. At one point, a protester challenged me to march with them if I truly felt how they did. I agreed to march and got a couple of officers to go with me for security purposes. As we took off down South Florissant Rd., I was happy to be leaving the police department because my real concern was that violence might erupt there. Unfortunately, we did not get very far before the crowd stopped, turned around, and headed back to the police department. Aside from verbal abuse and threats, the first several hours were uneventful, but we knew things would change as night fell.

The size of the crowd remained in the hundreds. Some of the earlier protestors had left, but new people had shown up for the night's events. Things had quieted down, and all the protestors had left the police department parking lot. They were all in the roadway or across the street. We could feel something was brewing, but we didn't know what. A group of officers stood on the front steps of the police department. More had gathered in the back parking lot, and the mobile field force units were out of sight.

I was inside the building—I don't remember why—when I heard chaos on the radio. Someone had thrown a commercial-grade firework at the officers in front of the building, and it had exploded in their midst. As the officers scattered for cover, rioters seized that moment to bum-rush the building with bats, crowbars, and metal pipes and began breaking the windows.

I raced down the hallway to the front of the building, where I heard the crescendo of shattering glass. I didn't know what was going on outside, but I assumed that people were trying to take over the building. There were civilian dispatchers inside the building, but I was the only officer. As I unholstered my firearm to defend myself and the dispatchers, I thought that my career was over. If I were forced to defend myself and innocent civilian workers from violent, armed rioters, that would not play out well in the public arena, but I was prepared to take whatever actions were necessary. I could envision the headline: *"Ferguson Police Chief Shoots and Kills Protester."* Thankfully, after a few seconds, the shattering stopped, and no one was entering the building. I snapped my firearm back into my holster and ran outside to see what was unfolding.

What I discovered was that we were under attack. In addition to the fireworks, frozen water bottles and softball-sized rocks were being hurled at the officers. I had given the call for mutual aid to be activated, but it was too late; the people intent on violence that evening had delivered the first blow, and they had destroyed the police department. We had to evacuate the dispatchers because it was no longer safe for them to be inside the building.

The tricky part about a protest that turns into civil unrest is that not everyone participates in the rioting. Some people are there just to watch the show. Unfortunately, several people were intent on violence and destruction that night. It turned out the reason they wanted to bust out the windows was so they could launch incendiary devices through them in hopes of starting a fire and burning the building down. Luckily, the fire department is right next door, and we were able to bring firefighters in through the back to extinguish the small blaze that had started inside the courtroom.

What transpired over the next several hours, I can only describe as a war zone. People continued to throw high-grade fireworks. Gunmen, hidden by the darkness of night, fired rounds at officers and the police department, and several officers were injured after being hit by flying objects or being too close to explosions. I commend the restraint of all of the officers who were victims of these heinous attacks. Despite being faced with deadly violence, we did not respond with deadly force because a lot of innocent people would have been in danger if we had done so. Ultimately, we decided to use tear gas, and that was extremely helpful in diffusing the assault against us.

The night's events ended around 3:00 a.m., and we were able to go home. Before leaving, I tried to muster up some words of encouragement for my officers because I was pretty sure we would face the same thing the next night. I don't recall what I said except that I was proud to stand alongside them in this effort.

After returning to an empty house in the wee hours of the morning, I was left to sit and reflect. I thought about what had happened with the attack and what I could have done differently, and I wondered if I was the right person to be leading this department. I was heartbroken for the people who had lived through the events in 2014 and were now facing a similar fate in 2020. I felt that I had failed them because I hadn't made the first move and activated additional resources before we were attacked. And what was I putting my family through? Most of the evening's events had played out on social media livestreams, so they had been able to see the chaos I'd been in the middle of. Needless to say, I couldn't sleep. I lay down around 4:00 a.m., and by 8:00 a.m., I was back at the police department.

Unfortunately, I was correct, and the rioters returned the next evening for another round of violence and destruction. The second night, we were much quicker to respond. As a result, we experienced fewer injuries to officers, and the police department was not damaged any further. The downside was that businesses in the area suffered more damage because we pushed the rioters away from the police department. Although still violent and destructive, Sunday night's events were not as bad as Saturday's.

By Monday night, the National Guard had been deployed to Ferguson, and we had another layer of resources. That night, we only saw protestors; the violent rioters had gone to downtown St. Louis. That night, four St. Louis police officers were shot (they all survived), and a retired St. Louis captain was shot and killed while working security at a pawn shop that was being looted.

In the weeks that followed, there were daily protests in Ferguson, but the violence and destruction had subsided. I didn't think any of the officers would stay at the department after that experience. After being the target of that level of violence for something you had nothing to do with, who would want to stick around and be subjected to that? To be honest, I was ready to leave the profession myself.

Some positives came from the chaos of the riots. Our officers were some of the first, if not the first, to take a knee in solidarity with protestors. That would go on to be a common theme throughout the protests around the globe. I was one of the first police chiefs in the country to march with George Floyd protestors, and that received a lot of positive feedback. Some folks, including some of my officers, were upset with me for doing so, but it felt like the right thing to do in the moment, and I have no regrets about making that decision.

We received a lot of positive press for how the unrest was handled compared to how it was handled in 2014. We engaged with protestors throughout the day, and despite being attacked, we did nothing to provoke or antagonize anyone. Our tactics were clearly in response to what we were facing, not our looking to dominate the community. In the weeks that followed, I actually received a letter of gratitude from someone who had been at the Kent State protest that had turned deadly in 1970.

Another positive that came from the protest was that we were able to engage with more people than before this tragedy happened. I received a call from the Ferguson-Florissant School District superintendent, Dr. Joseph S. Davis, who advised me that his students wanted to put on a Black Lives Matter march and rally in partnership with the police department. I agreed to the endeavor, and we provided road security as hundreds of students, parents, faculty, and community members marched through Ferguson in unity. I spoke at the rally and shared a message about the possibilities of change when you have leaders in a position to push the boundaries of what it can look like.

My teenage son, Jaxon, had come up for a visit during that time, and he and I walked together during the march. We used that time to talk about everything going on around the country, and I checked in with him about how he was feeling about what he had seen in the video. I also asked him about his feelings concerning what I was dealing with in Ferguson. I needed that time with him—probably more than he did.

Another call I received in the weeks after the riots was from a local pastor. This was not just any pastor, but a former NFL player and Pro Football Hall of Fame inductee, "Pastor A," and he called to ask me to meet with a young man. He explained that he had gone to one of the recent protests across the street from the police department. As the tension had risen among the protestors, this young man had interceded, and it was clear that he was a leader of the group. Pastor A struck up a conversation with this young man to learn what his motivation was for protesting. The young man had a problematic history with police officers and a very negative outlook on law enforcement because of his experiences. Pastor A told the young man that he believed he would benefit from a sit-down meeting with me and offered to coordinate it. We both agreed, and the three of us met one day at a private location away from the police department.

At the meeting, we had a pretty in-depth conversation, and the young man explained to me what his history was with police officers and why he felt we were inherently racist toward minorities. From the examples the young man shared, I would have had the same outlook as him if I had experienced what he had. The beauty of dialogue is that it is two-way communication. Just as the young man shared his story, I was able to share my story with him. I was able to share the things that we were doing to root out bad officers and how our reform efforts were positioning us to minimize the potential to have bad actors inside our organization. By the end of our conversation, the young man told Pastor A and me that he was glad he had agreed to the meeting. He said he'd never thought he would have any common ground with a police officer, but after our conversation, he felt that we had established just that.

After the George Floyd protests and riots, we were soon back in the planning stages for the Michael Brown anniversary. This time, I knew it was going to be different because tensions were so high across the nation from the deaths of George Floyd and Breanna Taylor. A different element would come out to protest that year, and it wouldn't be just the local crowd we'd experienced the year prior. I had decided that it wouldn't be a good idea for me to attend the memorial service that year—I really felt that my safety would be in jeopardy if I attended.

A few weeks before the anniversary, I received a letter in the mail from the Michael Brown Foundation. Not only were they asking me to attend the memorial service, but they were asking me to speak at it. Some highlights from the letter read, "Mr. & Mrs. Brown and the Michael Brown Foundation want to formally congratulate you on the great work you are doing in Ferguson... Your participation in our Memorial, as the Chief, will bridge the gap between the community and the change we want to see in Ferguson and the greater Metro area."

This gesture blew me away, and I was pissed at the same time because I really did not want to go down there. But I realized how big of a moment this was, not just for the police department and the local community but for the country. We had an opportunity to show the world what healing looked like when people committed to building bridges. I accepted the request to speak, and I attended the memorial, but this time, I took some officers with me for security.

On the day of the memorial, I had several contingencies in place for protection. Not only was I taking officers with me, but I had other staff monitoring the cameras in the area to be ready to send in additional help if things turned bad. To further confirm how bad of an idea it was for me to be there, as I was walking down the street to the memorial site, three individuals armed with AR-15s lined up across the street to block our path. I was familiar with the leader of the group, so I wasn't worried that they were going to use the weapons, but it highlighted how volatile my presence was at the memorial. After a brief conversation with the gun-toting intimidation crew, I made my way to the memorial site.

One thing I was worried about was that the news coverage would be about me and my comments as opposed to the family and impacted loved ones. I did not have a prepared speech—as with most public remarks, I relied on my heart and the feeling of the space I was in to provide the motivation for what I would say. I talked about the impact of the events from that day six years earlier and how we were still working today to ensure we were doing everything we could to continuously move toward positive change. I kept my remarks short and accomplished my goal of not getting booed by those in attendance.

As I stood in place to watch the rest of the service, I found myself in a conversation with the leader of the event security team. I was familiar with this person because he was always armed at protests, but we had never met before. We had a really good conversation about the state of affairs in Ferguson and policing in general. I will always remember his last words to me. He stated that I had earned his respect for showing up and spending time with them at the memorial. I took that as my reward for being willing to step outside of my comfort zone and attend an event I was concerned my presence would be triggering. What that moment highlighted for me was the power of meeting people where they are.

Later that evening, we would have a tense protest and standoff at the police department. Some of the same people who had been pleasant with me just hours earlier were now cursing me and verbally abusing my officers. The night was long, but there was no significant violence. Destruction was minimal compared to what we had experienced a couple of months earlier. Despite the challenges of the day, we made it through another anniversary.

At that point, I was in survival mode—not survival for my job, but survival for me and my family. The span of events from COVID-19 in February through the George Floyd riots in May and June and to the anniversary in August was easily the toughest stretch of my life. I've only covered the highlights. I haven't gone into the internal challenges and community struggles; those are for later chapters.

Two more events shaped my remaining time in Ferguson. The first was watching the insurrection footage in my office on January 6. It was difficult and emotionally draining. I had flashbacks to the May 30 protest, which had erupted in violence and destruction. Seeing what our country had become was sickening, and I struggled to find hope for better days. The second event was the trial of Dereck Chauvin in April of 2021. We knew that if he were not convicted for killing George Floyd, we would likely experience rioting again in Ferguson. I was sitting in my office when the verdict was read, and when they said "guilty," I started to cry.

I got so emotional for two reasons. The first was relief: My department was going to be spared from living through the nightmare of violence and destruction that would have been sure to come if he had been found not guilty. The second was validation: What we saw in the video was wrong, and people were united on that.

My life in Ferguson had become so crazy that I realized I could not handle the impact it was having on me and my family. I hit rock bottom one day when my wife told me what my five-year-old daughter had asked her: "Mommy, how come Daddy is never happy when he sees us when he gets home?" Every ounce of me was being drained from me at work, and I had nothing of quality left to give my family. At that moment, I knew I needed to leave Ferguson before it cost me more than I was willing to sacrifice. In August 2021, I returned to my home state of North Carolina to take on my next challenge in Apex, NC.

CHAPTER 4

THE COMMUNITY

Sir Robert Peel is considered the "father of modern policing" for establishing the Metropolitan Police Force in London, England, in 1829. Peel is famously known for his nine policing principles, which are just as applicable today as they were in the 1800s, if not more. I'm not going to go into all nine, but I want to highlight several:

- *Principle Two*: "To recognize always that the power of the police to fulfill their functions and duties is dependent on public approval of their existence, actions and behavior, and on their ability to secure and maintain public respect."

- *Principle Three*: "To recognize always that to secure and maintain the respect and approval of the public also means the securing of the willing cooperation of the public in the task of securing observance of laws."

- *Principle Four*: "To recognize always that the extent to which the cooperation of the public can be secured diminishes proportionately the necessity of the use of physical force and compulsion for achieving police objectives."

- *Principle Six*: "To use physical force only when the exercise of persuasion, advice and warning is found to be insufficient to obtain public cooperation to an extent necessary to secure observance of law or to restore order, and to use only the minimum degree of physical force which is necessary on any particular occasion for achieving a police objective."

- *Principle Seven*: "To maintain at all times a relationship with the public that gives reality to the historic tradition that the police are the public and that the public is the police, the police being only members of the public who are paid to give full-time attention to duties which are incumbent on every citizen in the interests of community welfare and existence."

After reading through these principles, I'm pretty confident that most people would agree with Peel's assessment of how the police need to interact and engage with the communities they serve.

Most law enforcement professionals are familiar with Peel's principles or have at least heard them a time or two. They are often referenced in law enforcement training classes or even presentations to community groups. However, in America, when you talk about the origins of policing, depending on who your audience is, you may get a very different response. The NAACP has an information page on its website titled "The Origins of Modern-Day Policing."[2] An excerpt from this page says, "The origins of modern-day policing can be traced back to the 'Slave Patrol.' The earliest formal slave patrol was created in the Carolinas in the early 1700s with one mission: to establish a system of terror and squash slave uprisings with the capacity to pursue, apprehend, and return runaway slaves to their owners."

The NAACP is not the only entity that felt it was important to highlight the significance of America's complicated past of "policing." One of the most respected and visible law enforcement entities is the National

---

[2] https://naacp.org/find-resources/history-explained/origins-modern-day-policing.

Law Enforcement Officers Memorial Fund (NLEOMF). Their website states: "The purpose of the National Law Enforcement Officers Memorial Fund is to honor the role of law enforcement, in service to society, by recognizing the sacrifices and valor of law enforcement, educating the community, and making it safer for those who serve."[3] It's safe to say that you would be hard-pressed to find a bigger supporter of law enforcement than NLEOMF.

The organization's website contains an article titled "Slave Patrols: An Early Form of American Policing," which shares the oath that slave patrollers in North Carolina swore to: "I [patroller's name], do swear, that I will as searcher for guns, swords, and other weapons among the slaves in my district, faithfully, and as privately as I can, discharge the trust reposed in me as the law directs, to the best of my power. So help me, God."[4]

This dilemma of the origins of modern-day policing highlights the complexities of the challenges we face in many communities. As I mentioned earlier, watching the fallout in Ferguson was a wake-up call for me to get more engaged in the community, and my first step was to organize and host a town hall event. I was a captain at the time in Forest Park. I'm a member of the National Organization of Black Law Enforcement Executives (NOBLE), and I found myself leading a committee that was tasked with putting on this event. Since I was heading up the committee, I opted to host it in Forest Park.

Overall, the town hall meeting was a success. We had community members, elected officials, police department leadership, and outside law enforcement personnel there, all speaking from their perspectives on matters related to law enforcement and the community. What was noteworthy for me was that a couple of our council members who were

---

[3] https://nleomf.org/.
[4] https://nleomf.org/slave-patrols-an-early-form-of-american-policing/.

outspoken about their dislike of our police department complimented us for hosting the event and opening up the space for dialogue.

After this event, I was hooked, and I wanted to do more to bring people from the community and law enforcement together and build bridges. When I looked at the work that needed to be done in the community, the area I focused on was teens. I ended up connecting with the football and basketball coaches at Forest Park High School. For the football team, I conducted a Law & Your Community presentation. NOBLE's Law & Your Community "is a nationally recognized hands-on interactive training program for young people ages 13–18 designed to improve their communications with law enforcement officers and their understanding of their federal, state, and local laws."[5] I also attended some of the team's events and activities. I had played semi-pro football several years earlier, so I used my football experience as a connection point to build rapport with them.

The basketball coach actually let me practice with the varsity team. Although I played basketball in college, I had no business being on the court with those fast-running, high-flying kids, but in my head, I could still compete with anyone. I would see some of the kids around the city, and they would speak to me because they had gotten to interact with me in a non-law enforcement capacity. I didn't show up in their world because something was wrong; I showed up to build relationships before anything wrong ever happened. I hoped to educate and resonate with as many of them as possible so that they avoided "the wrong" and never had to deal with law enforcement on that level.

A highlight for me at that time was when the football team was recognized at a council meeting. The team's star, "JE," was tasked with giving some remarks on behalf of the team, and he mentioned me in his

---

[5] https://noblenational.org/the-law-and-your-community/.

remarks. In my eyes, I wasn't doing anything special, but the kids appreciated the fact that I showed up and engaged with them. As a side note, JE went on to play at an SEC school and got drafted into the NFL.

Every community is made up of unique people who contribute to its dynamics. Unfortunately, sometimes, community members turn to criminal activity as their contribution. Not everything in bridge-building is outreach and engagement; sometimes, it's crime-fighting as well.

Rosetown was a neighborhood in Forest Park that had a history of illegal drug activity. It was predominantly black, and unfortunately, because of the actions of a few, the entire neighborhood was looked at with skepticism by a lot of officers in the department. I did a lot of enforcement work in Rosetown, especially while in the special operations unit. Although I was committed to rooting out the illegal element in Rosetown, I was also committed to treating people with dignity and fairness. Just because I was taking someone to jail for selling drugs, it didn't mean I had to be disrespectful or discourteous to them.

One of the regulars in Rosetown whom I arrested several times over the years told me one day that he respected me for how I conducted business. He said they all knew to be looking over their shoulder if they were up to no good because I was always lurking, but he appreciated how I dealt with them when I caught them. He even credited my relentlessness as motivation for him to clean his life up. Just because a person is in a down season of life, it doesn't mean they will stay there. You never know how your treatment of them can help them navigate those tough seasons of life.

As I continued to look for ways to engage with the community, one day, I saw a social media post from a police chief in North Carolina. The post was about a meeting between officers and community members at a barbershop. I was intrigued by this setup, and I reached out to the chief to learn more about what they were doing. The chief explained to me that a neighboring police department was actually running the program in partnership with a community member. I eventually got in contact with the community member, Tru Pettigrew, and he explained how they ran the Barbershop Rap Sessions program and what the payoffs had been since its inception. Eventually, I rolled out a barbershop program in Forest Park, a blend of the Barbershop Rap Session and The Law & Your Community presentation. This new initiative was a huge success for me and the department.

Two things happened in the weeks after the first barbershop event. The first was that longtime Forest Park resident Mr. F came to the next council meeting and spoke during public comments. Mr. F thanked us for hosting the barbershop event and stated that we should have been doing that type of engagement years ago.

The second thing that happened was, one day, we were looking for a suspect we had tracked to a residence. The suspect was inside but would not communicate with us and would not come out. These are often the worst situations for law enforcement to handle. Things are much easier and safer if the suspect surrenders and allows themselves to be taken into custody. These situations are dangerous because we do not know what is waiting for us on the other side of the door. We don't know if the person is just scared and is hiding or if they are armed and have the mindset that they are not going to jail and will resort to violence.

I was at the scene. As we were preparing our strategy, a gentleman walked up and told me that he had been at the barbershop event we'd just had. It turned out that the suspect was a relative of his. This gentleman had been in communication with his relative, and he claimed that the suspect would give up without a fight. We used the family member to communicate with the suspect, and we were able to get him into custody without having to use force or anyone getting hurt. The gentleman explained to me afterward that he felt comfortable working with me to resolve the incident because of the impression he'd gotten from the barbershop event. I was now seeing firsthand how community engagement was helping with police matters and activity. It was a great feeling to know that engagement efforts had led to the safe resolution of a situation that could have ended much worse.

Community outreach in Forest Park was very different from what I experienced in Ferguson. In Forest Park, I was trying to build relationships before the crisis happened, which is much easier to do. In Ferguson, I was trying to build relationships and partnerships after the crisis and chaos had already impacted the community and the police department in a major way. Ideally, this is not where you want to be, but if this is where you find yourself, you have to navigate this dynamic in the best way possible.

Before the crisis or critical incident disrupts the community, you want to see how your community is set up and what you are doing to engage and interact with them. Do you hear their concerns and their issues? Do they have a way to convey what they need from you, what they want to see from you? How are you all working together to address those things? The more work you do on the front end before you ever have that crisis, the more it will pay off if you find yourself in the midst of a crisis. It doesn't mean that you're not going to have protests or riots, but it helps to have friends and partners to support you in those tough times. You only build that up through being intentional in your outreach and engagement efforts.

This approach is not only applicable to law enforcement. Any business that needs the support of the community should approach their work in this manner. I once saw a developer come into a community and engage with the people before they started their project. They got to meet the community leaders and learn about its nuances. They learned what the community wanted from them so they could plan how to develop things the community needed and wanted and, at the same time, make the company and their business partners money.

If you have ever attended one of my training classes, you've probably heard me talk about "Community PIE." Community PIE is my formula for achieving the best results in community outreach and engagement. It's important to note that, on their own, community outreach and engagement do not equal community policing. While they are components of community policing—and critical ones—as a whole, community policing is focused on impacting crime.

In 2019, I served on the International Association of Chiefs of Police (IACP) community policing committee. That year, we got a resolution passed by the IACP to adopt an official definition of community policing. It reads: "Community policing is a comprehensive philosophy that guides policy and strategy aimed at achieving more effective and efficient crime control, reduced fear of crime, improved quality of life, and improved police services and police legitimacy through a proactive reliance on community resources that seeks to change crime causing conditions. This assumes a need for greater accountability of police, elected community leaders, and the community in general, along with greater public share in decision-making through the identification of service needs and priorities and a greater concern for civil rights and liberties."[6]

...a commitment to building partnerships with a wide range of community stakeholders coupled with an emphasis on being innovative to explore new ways of doing things and empowering both community and law enforcement to create in the same space is the recipe for success.

---

[6] "Crime Prevention, Domestic Security and Quality of Life: Definition and Significant Value of Community Policing," https://www.theiacp.org/resources/resolution/crime-prevention-domestic-security-and-quality-of-life-definition-and.

To achieve community policing success, you have to build relationships with the people in your community. You do that through outreach and engagement, and you do that more effectively when you follow the practice of Community PIE.

Community PIE stands for Partnerships, Innovation, and Empowerment. I use PIE because who doesn't like pie? What I've learned in working in different communities around the country is that a commitment to building partnerships with a wide range of community stakeholders coupled with an emphasis on being innovative to explore new ways of doing things and empowering both community and law enforcement to create in the same space is the recipe for success.

> *When I learn of community members who are skeptical of law enforcement, I try to find ways to get them engaged with the department so they can truly learn about us and what we do.*

One area in which I have been highly successful is partnering with individuals or groups who do not like or have had a difficult history with law enforcement. When I learn of community members who are skeptical of law enforcement, I try to find ways to get them engaged with the department so they can truly learn about us and what we do. Too often, officers are quick to write someone off if they are critical of law enforcement. They are often labeled "anti-police," and if you are labeled that, the police dislike you just as much as you dislike them.

I've had to navigate these dynamics at just about every stop on my law enforcement journey. What I can say is that by using the community PIE approach, I have partnered with people who never thought they would partner with the police on anything. I have used community activists to assist me with assessing candidates for law enforcement executive positions.

At times, I have been criticized by department members for my willingness to bring in these individuals. My philosophy in this area is simple. If our biggest critics are able to build trust in what we are doing or where we are headed as an organization, who will be left to criticize us? I can always find or create a way to engage with someone willing to engage, regardless of what their views of me or my department are. I have the confidence that if they truly see us, they will naturally grow to appreciate what it is we do.

I once learned of a police department that put together a children's book for elementary school kids in the community. In this book, they highlighted some of the officers from the department so the kids could read and learn about the people who worked in their community. I thought that was a pretty cool idea, so I assigned my staff to reach out to this department and get a copy of their book. Once we saw what their book looked like, I wanted my department to put out one, too.

Now, what I have described thus far shows no innovation on my or my agency's part. We learned of someone else's idea and wanted to replicate it. But I didn't just want to replicate it; I wanted to find a way to make it stand out and have a bigger impact. I didn't know what I was looking for to make that happen, but luckily, I have great people with creative minds in my organization, and one of them had an excellent idea. They recommended we put blank autograph pages in the back of the book. That way, kids could carry them around and collect autographs from our officers. I loved this idea, and that is exactly what we did with the book.

To announce the book to the community, I did a video for social media. In the video, I encouraged kids to collect autographs from all of our officers because it would make them feel special. The autograph pages were the only innovative part of the book, but they were the most impactful because they drove engagement and interaction with the youth in the community. It was an immediate hit. The community loved the idea and what we were trying to do. Local media picked up the book initiative, and they did a story on it.

A couple of months later, I was contacted by a producer from *Good Morning America 3* because they were looking to do a positive law enforcement story, and they had learned of our book. A little creativity was sprinkled onto an existing idea—and look at the magic that ensued.

Every organization, no matter the profession, is full of thinkers with wide ranging imaginations. When you have an organization full of people with imaginations and ideas, you have to empower them to bring those ideas forward. I have to admit that this is harder than it sounds. As the leader of an organization, I'm often responsible for saying yes or no to suggestions and recommendations. When your idea receives a no, that can discourage you from putting another idea forward. As leaders, we have to be mindful of how we dish out our no's because we don't want to squash the empowerment mindset of our people.

I have regularly challenged my staff to come up with engagement initiatives that they can implement themselves. My only requirement is that it has to be something that everyone on the team can participate in. From those simple instructions, I've seen some amazing creativity come forward, things that I would never have thought to do. One of my patrol teams created a program in partnership with a local church to supply resource bags for people they encountered who were going through tough times. These bags were made available to the entire department so everyone had access to them if they encountered someone who needed the resource.

Another idea was for the department to host a puzzle exchange. I had never heard of anything like this and was intrigued to learn more. I discovered that there is a network of individuals who meet up and exchange jigsaw puzzles. One of my officers was part of this network and shared how uncomfortable it could be to meet up with a stranger to exchange a puzzle, so they thought it would be a good idea if we hosted an exchange that could be done safely at the police department. We hosted our first exchange event on a Saturday morning, and almost three hundred people walked through the doors of the police department that day to exchange puzzles. I could have never envisioned we would have that level of turnout for a puzzle exchange, but that just goes to show that empowering people to contribute to the ideas of the organization will benefit the organization and the community.

One of my all-time favorite engagement events was organizing a birthday parade for a little girl in Ferguson. As the chief, I try to get out when I can and show my officers that I'm willing to assist them when needed. On this particular day, I was driving back to the police department when I saw one of my officers handling an accident in the roadway, and traffic was backed up. I was wearing a suit that day, as opposed to a uniform. Nevertheless, I stopped, put on my traffic vest, and assisted with directing traffic until the traffic had cleared.

While I was out there, the window of a passing car rolled down, and the driver asked me if I was the chief. I said yes, and she asked me if I would do a birthday parade for her daughter. She went on to explain to me that her daughter, Paydenn, was about to turn six and was battling a rare form of stage-four cancer. My daughter was six at the time, and I remember thinking how devastated I would be if she were facing a challenge like that. This was during the height of COVID-19, and with Paydenn's weakened immune system, she couldn't be around too many people.

I agreed to do the parade and got to work recruiting others to join in on the effort. Soon, I had media coverage and several other police and fire departments all committed to be in the parade. I had elected officials come out for it, and car clubs joined in, too. It turned into a complete community support effort. I even remember seeing some of our local activists out there, who typically did not come to events we spearheaded.

On the day of the event, a local restaurant owner brought his food truck and fed everyone participating in the parade for free. The parade was a huge success. Paydenn had the biggest smile when she saw all the vehicles and people who had come out just for her. Many people brought gifts for her. The family had a GoFundMe account for medical costs, and it received a much-needed boost from the media coverage. Secondary to how great the day was for Paydenn, I met and engaged with a host of new community members I didn't know before that day. People got to see firsthand what the Ferguson Police Department was all about. It wasn't just about enforcing laws and chasing down bad guys. It was about being a good partner in the community and being there to support the community in any way we could. When people start to see your organization in that light, the future is bright.

I started this chapter by talking about the origins of modern policing. In many communities where there is a lack of trust in police, there is often a history attached to those feelings. For me, the most noteworthy component of connecting with the community is having an understanding of its history, particularly the role that policing has played. Before going to Ferguson, I was not aware of the historical racial challenges and dynamics of the area. Ferguson was a sundown town in the 1930s. For those not familiar with the term, that meant that blacks had to be out of Ferguson before it got dark or they would face consequences, often violent ones.

Ferguson borders a city called Kinloch, which was the first African-American incorporated city in Missouri. I watched a documentary on the relationship between Ferguson and Kinloch back in the day. The documentary highlighted that the main street connecting the two towns, Suburban Ave, had been blocked off and barricaded for decades by Ferguson, though there are varying accounts as to why.[7] Needless to say, the black Kinloch residents felt it was done to prevent or dissuade them from

---

[7] PBS, "Where the Pavement Ends," *America Reframed*,
https://www.pbs.org/video/where-the-pavement-ends-5eg5k8/.

coming to Ferguson. The barricade was put up in the late 1940s or early 1950s and was taken down in the 1970s after protests over its existence.

Michael Brown was shot and killed in Southeast Ferguson. During the DOJ investigation, many residents from that part of town expressed a feeling of not being a part of Ferguson. Southeast Ferguson is situated between the cities of Dellwood and Jennings. Some people in that area felt as though they were more a part of one of those cities instead of Ferguson. Canfield Dr., where Michael Brown was shot and killed, is to the east of West Florissant Rd. That area of Ferguson is home to a group of apartment complexes that are all adjacent to one another, with only a couple of streets having single-family homes. Another factor is that the kids who live in that part of Ferguson do not attend school in the Ferguson-Florissant School District. Instead, they are zoned for the Riverview Gardens School District.

Why is all of this relevant? Because it helps us understand the rage and frustration that exploded after Darren Wilson killed Michael Brown. When people don't feel like they are part of the community, and there are historical accounts that highlight the notion that people who looked like them were not wanted in the town from the beginning, that impact cannot be ignored. Those are the historical obstacles that we have to overcome in the present day to build the community relationships that are needed for true healing.

Community PIE helps us overcome some of the historical barriers that contribute to the dynamic of police-community relationships. My best PIE moment was birthed out of a random meeting at a men's church event with a gentleman who goes by DT. During the service, the pastor instructed us to turn to our neighbor and engage in whatever instructions the pastor had for us. That random encounter led to a conversation between DT and me, where he learned that I was the police chief in Ferguson, and I learned that he wanted to start a mentoring program for the youth in the area.

Soon after that encounter, DT invited me to the kickoff meeting for Boys 2 MenTORRs (Teaching Others Respect and Responsibility). In brainstorming ways to connect youths to law enforcement, we talked about having a basketball game. I was responsible for getting officers to the gym, and DT was responsible for getting youths from the community there. The event was called "Ballin' with a Cop." The beauty of it was that the bulk of the kids who came to play had no idea they were playing against police officers. I admit that we lost the game—it was rigged—but afterward, we sat the kids down and mentored them, and that is when they learned that they had just finished playing against police officers. After the event, we had food for the kids, and we just hung around talking smack to each other about what had happened in the game.

Sounds pretty simple, right? Well, here is the part that highlights the impact of connecting with community partners. About three months after our first Ballin' with a Cop event, I was at work in Southeast Ferguson. I was in uniform and driving my unmarked police vehicle. While driving around, I saw one of the kids from the basketball game. I stopped and called out to him to get his attention. I was behind him, so he had to turn around to look at me, and when we made eye contact, I didn't see what I normally did when I was in uniform and called out to a young person I wanted to talk to. I didn't see any hesitation in his eyes, and there was no fight-or-flight response kicking in. What I saw was recognition. We went on to have a short conversation; mainly, I was just checking on him to see how things were going. I had been introduced to this young man through non-enforcement activities, and now I was engaging with him in uniform, but it didn't matter. That's the power of community PIE, so get some PIE in your life.

In November 1952, a young man by the name of Lynn Council was picked up along with several other young black males and brought in for questioning by Apex Police Chief Sam Bagwell. According to Mr. Council, the chief beat him in hopes of getting a confession from him for a convenience store robbery that had happened in another jurisdiction. Mr. Council had nothing to do with the robbery, so he had no confession to give. After being transferred to the Wake County Jail, Mr. Council found himself being removed from his cell by Chief Bagwell and put in a car with two deputy sheriffs. Those deputies drove Mr. Council out into a field, tied a noose around his neck, and hung him from a tree. They hung him there for approximately a minute before letting him down. Mr. Council was released from custody the next day and would keep this experience silent for decades before he felt comfortable enough to share it publicly. I had the honor of meeting Mr. Council in 2023 as the first black police chief of Apex. While I had nothing to do with the atrocity that Mr. Council was exposed to, I still felt compelled to apologize to him on behalf of the Apex Police Department.

These are just some of the community traumas that have been passed down from generation to generation and have had a significant impact on our community relationships today. I've met with people who have flat-out told me to my face that there is nothing that can be done to get them to willingly interact with the police, let alone trust the police.

Whether the people love the police, hate the police, or feel something in between, we need them to be engaged and connected to what we are trying to do.

I had a community member tell me one time that the police don't care anything about anyone in the community but themselves. His reason for this is that when one community member kills another, the police put up some crime scene tape, ask people if they saw anything, and, after a short time, pack up and leave. But when a police officer is seriously hurt or killed, we shut everything down, bring in hundreds of officers to help and don't rest until we have hunted the person down. Until that conversation, I had never thought about how the community might view the police's response to an officer being killed compared to the response when a community member is killed, but they are two very different responses.

Communities are very different, although there are often many similarities, too. For law enforcement to have the best chance to be successful at building bridges in the community, they have to be intentional about engaging with all its facets. Whether the people love the police, hate the police, or feel something in between, we need them to be engaged and connected to what we are trying to do. Sir Robert Peel gave us the blueprint all those years ago, and we are still trying to bring those principles to fruition.

CHAPTER 5

THE WHY

The first time I met with the chief who hired me in Forest Park, I told him that I wanted to be the chief one day. I couldn't explain why I wanted this; I just knew it was an important position and seemed like a cool thing to aspire to become. If you are someone who is looking to take on the challenge of leadership, you should be able to answer emphatically when asked, "What is your *why?*"

For some leaders, there is one momentous experience that fueled their desire to want to lead, and they can answer that question very easily. For others, like me, it is a culmination of events and experiences that build the desire to lead. The question that police officers get asked most often is, "Why did you become a police officer?" If I'm answering that question honestly, I became a police officer for the money. Not for the money, as in my police salary, but the $30,000 I mentioned in Chapter 1 that came with my participation in the police corps program. That incentive was the primary driver for me considering policing; before that, I solely had my sights set on being a special agent at the federal level.

Once I explain to people my "$30k motivation," I tell them that asking me why I became a police officer is not the appropriate question. The proper question is, "Why did you *stay* a police officer?" My answer to that question is very simple: I recognized that I was needed in the profession, and I felt uniquely positioned to have a positive impact.

Earlier, I mentioned my time in the V.I.P.E.R. Unit. One of the best parts about being on that team was working undercover details. As a young officer, it was always cool when I was able to wear plain clothes to work instead of my uniform. One thing that was noteworthy for me at this time was that I did not have the money to buy undercover clothes, and the city did not provide a clothing allowance, either. So, when I showed up to work in plain clothes, they were my regular clothes that I wore outside of work. I was in my mid-20s at the time, and I dressed very urban, or what would be labeled "hip hop." When I started coming to the police station in my regular clothes, a lot of officers would joke with me about my attire. In a completely joking manner, they would make comments like, "Who let the thug in here?" and "How did the hoodlum get past security?" There weren't many young black males working there, and I clearly stood out with how I dressed.

One place where my attire fit in very well was out in the community. That's what made me good at undercover work: I had "the look," and I didn't give off a law enforcement vibe. But after a while, as the officers continued to joke about my attire, I started to recognize that it might be problematic when it came to the people who dressed and looked like me out in the community. It was all part of police banter; these people were friends and colleagues of mine, and I didn't take anything they were saying to me as being disrespectful. But my concern grew with the notion that the sight of a young black male dressed in urban clothes automatically triggered the thought that he was a "thug" or "hoodlum." If that's what they thought when they saw me, how did they view young black males who dressed or looked like me, whom they did not know?

During this time, the term "implicit bias" had not become a buzzword in the policing profession, but clearly, that was what I was seeing in the individuals who always had a joke for me. I can't stress enough that these were not bad people; these were not people I felt were racist or anything remotely on that level. My initial approach to addressing this bias was a passive one. One thing that separated me from many of my colleagues back then was the fact that I had a college degree. I used that to launch my passive counter to the biased comments I received. An example of such an exchange would go something like this:

"Who let the thug in here?"

"This thug is smarter and more educated than you are!"

Probably not the best approach to address this issue, but that's all I had to offer at the time. Over the years, I matured and got promoted, which gave me a different outlook on how I could make an impact. I now had influence over the officers I directly supervised. I started to use that influence to educate them on things that might come across as disrespectful or offensive if they didn't have a good understanding of the different community dynamics at play. I also started to find my voice with my peers and supervisors to where I was getting more comfortable having conversations about sensitive matters and being the educator in the room, especially if I was the only minority present, which was often. The higher I climbed, the more comfortable I felt being the person who said what needed to be said. As things got more and more complicated with the policing profession, that evolved into my "why."

With this added influence came responsibility. I admit, I didn't fully understand the responsibility at first. Luckily, I had people on my team who felt comfortable enough with me to share their thoughts and feelings on matters that bothered them. One issue that was brought to my attention involved an online training class I had assigned my team to take. The class focused on implicit bias. I didn't just assign it to my team; I took the class as well. I found the class informative, and there was nothing earth-shattering about the content. However, the content landed very differently for my white officers. After completing the training, one of them approached me and asked not to be assigned another class like the one I had chosen. This officer explained that their takeaway from the training was that it felt like they were being shamed for being white.

I was shocked to hear this, but I was glad I was hearing it. I checked with another one of my white officers to see if they felt the same way and yes, they did. Instead of resonating with the teaching points in the class, the training had turned them off and they got little value out of it. That was certainly not my intent, but this taught me a valuable lesson. I did not receive the training how they did because it didn't impact me how it impacted them. I needed to be more mindful and intentional about forecasting the impacts that actions have. I learned to better scrutinize training to find a healthy balance of what was needed to reach desired outcomes. This is the method I use in delivering my training classes, especially my bias training.

The death of Trayvon Martin in 2012 and the national attention it got had more impact on me than anything that had happened previously in my career. Although that incident did not involve a police officer, the nation talked about George Zimmerman as if he were associated with law enforcement—so much so that I received a letter from a seventh grader that referenced the police killing of Trayvon Martin. I worked it out with the principal of the school and was able to visit with her class and have a discussion about police-community dynamics. I also educated her on the Trayvon Martin incident and the fact that George Zimmerman was not a police officer, which she appreciated.

The Trayvon incident was the first time I did a lot of talking to people about the complexities of criminal cases. I remember this case being heavily talked about among my friends, who are mostly non-law enforcement. Since I had a decade of experience in the profession by that time, people wanted to hear my take on the matter. I thought what had happened to

Trayvon was tragic, but I didn't think Zimmerman would be convicted of the charges he was facing. I told everyone that the elements of the charges didn't match up to what could be argued or proven in court. I feel George Zimmerman was reckless in his decision-making in that situation and unnecessarily put himself in the position to have a physical altercation with Trayvon. Although Zimmerman should not have done what he did, I felt strongly that he would be found not guilty because I didn't see the evidence to support the charges against him.

Some people, even friends, had a problem with me saying that. It was almost like because I was black, I had to root for Zimmerman to be found guilty. I understood the sensitivity of the race component that was at play for the nation as we followed the trial, but that didn't and wouldn't prevent me from speaking on a matter from my professional perspective. I thought of myself as trying to lessen the blow of disappointment for people by prepping them for the not-guilty verdict, but in the end, people felt how they felt, and that was a good learning lesson for me in navigating these sensitive matters.

Unfortunately, after the Trayvon incident, we would see multiple cases across the country where black individuals died at the hands of the police. Each of these incidents, regardless of the circumstances surrounding them, caused more and more problems for the relationships between law enforcement and the community, the black community in particular. As someone who lived in both worlds, I felt conflicted at times because, depending on which group I was with, I often had to advocate for the other group. If I were among police officers, I'd be fighting for an understanding of the black community. If I were among black people, I'd fight for an understanding of law enforcement.

One person who helped me better understand how to navigate that dynamic was my long-time friend "V." She and I have known each other since high school and have grown to be like family. V's life journey took her on the route of a community activist and advocate, while my life journey took me to law enforcement, but we have remained extremely close through it all. We have had some very intense arguments about police actions at multiple levels. V often tries to drill the community argument into my brain while I try to drill the police argument into hers. The beauty of our relationship is that we have never argued from a place of anger toward each other. I understand her commitment to activism; she understands my commitment to law enforcement, and we have always found unity in wanting better for communities that have strained relationships with law enforcement.

I've learned two critical lessons from my discussions with V over the years. The first is the significance of what law enforcement says publicly after an incident, particularly an officer's use of force where there is a death or serious injury. V would point out examples of when the comments from law enforcement leaders after a tragic incident fueled the response of activists. They weren't negative comments, but they lacked empathy and sensitivity, and that's why they were so damaging to people in the community. The second lesson is how community members feel about the system—or the lack thereof.

V and I had one of our most intense square-offs after a recent incident. I often call for patience, for the incident to be investigated, and for the facts to come out so everyone has a clearer picture of what happened and can form their own opinions on the actions of everyone involved. V explained that in her world, the activist world, they have no trust in the process playing out because it doesn't seem to them that there is a true system to hold law enforcement accountable. She said that if a community member shoots and kills another community member, everyone in the community knows what is going to happen. The police are going to track that person down and try to put them in jail as soon as possible. But when the police shoot and kill someone, even if there is a video to support how problematic it is, the officer knows they are going home that night. That's why activists don't typically wait for the facts of the case to come out before taking to the streets in protest. She explained that until a system was put in place that they had confidence in, the protest response would typically be the same.

I did not realize it at the time, but all of the conversations I was having with family, friends, and coworkers were building up my bank of knowledge. That would prove invaluable as I started to step more into the arena of community bridge-building. As I mentioned earlier, when I started being vocal about this topic in my organization, it was not received so well, but I saw the value in it. My belief that this was my path and my contribution to the profession continued to grow. Although I didn't have a lot of power and authority to effect significant change, at that time, I could take small steps that would get me to where I was trying to go.

One way was through NOBLE's Law & Your Community presentation, which I mentioned earlier. The training is designed to lead a dialogue with community members, especially teens, to help them understand laws and how to better interact with law enforcement, which was just what we needed. By the time I was facilitating this training, the country had experienced the bulk of the high-profile police-related incidents that almost everyone is familiar with. We had seen Michael Brown in Ferguson, Eric Garner in New York, Freddy Gray in Baltimore, Alton Sterling in Baton Rouge, Philando Castile in Minnesota, Tamir Rice in Cleveland, and Sandra Bland in Texas. The Sandra Bland incident was one of the most difficult to navigate at the time because there were a lot of conspiracy theories as to what led up to her being found dead in her jail cell from an apparent suicide.

As a result of this community trauma playing out for the world to see, we had a huge uphill battle to win the trust of our communities. When presenting Law & Your Community, at the very beginning of the presentation, I would ask the audience, "Who hates the police?" On average, about 80% or more of the people in the room would stick their hands up. My follow-up to that question would be, "Lower your hand if you've never had a direct interaction with a police officer." Without fail, over half the hands raised would go down. That told me that the bulk of the people who didn't like law enforcement got their negative perceptions through the experiences of others, like family or friends, or through viral content on the news and social media. I saw all those hands going down as people who would probably change their outlook if they had a positive experience with law enforcement. I saw myself as someone who could lead that positive experience, and that became my "*why.*"

Being the person to lead positive interactions with community members was only half the battle. I needed to do more work in the profession to get others to see the benefit of building relationships with the community. I mentioned earlier that my first agency was big on traffic enforcement. There is nothing wrong with traffic enforcement when the actions of those committing violations warrant it. Enforcement becomes problematic when it is used as a funding source. I can't say with any certainty that the financial component drove my first agency, but it felt that way to me at times.

When I told people where I worked, they often commented that they avoided driving through Forest Park because they knew they would get stopped if they did. Now, if someone were a hardened criminal, of course, I would want them to avoid my city. But these were not hardened criminals; most of these people were not criminals of any kind. Hearing that repeatedly hurt, but I had to use that hurt to lead change.

One thing that I did not get a chance to change in Forest Park was how we ran license plate checks. I have never been a fan of officers randomly running the license plate of a vehicle "just because." The law allows officers to do that because there is no expectation of privacy since the license plate has to be publicly displayed. But I feel it makes it too easy for bias to creep into the mix and influence what plates an officer chooses to run.

As the on-duty captain in Forest Park one day, I received a phone call from a woman who was upset that an officer had just followed her vehicle. She explained that she had been driving down the street, and the officer had pulled out behind her and followed her for a decent amount of time. She wanted to know why the officer was harassing her. She said, "I know he was checking my tag." She wanted an answer as to why the officer had gotten behind her, and I told her I would check into the matter and call her back.

From the location she'd given me, I had a pretty good idea of which officer had been driving behind her. I gave the officer a call and asked if he had followed her vehicle, and he admitted that he had. I asked him why, and he explained that he had been checking the license plate. When I asked what reason he had to check the license plate, he answered that he didn't have one. Since I couldn't defend his actions with that explanation, I gave him the woman's phone number and instructed him to call her and explain himself. I never asked him what explanation he gave her, but I doubt it was as simple as "I ran your tag because I can." I explained to that officer that I couldn't order him to stop doing that because the department allowed it, but he would have to explain himself to callers because I wouldn't defend it. I never got another call about that officer following people for no apparent reason.

Over the years, so many people have complained to me about being harassed by officers following behind them. Even if they don't get pulled over, they often feel the officer is trying to find something wrong with their vehicle so they can pull them over, and that is traumatic for them.

Instead of walking out the door thinking about how many tickets they needed to write, I wanted officers to think about how they could positively impact the community.

When I became the interim chief of Forest Park, one of the first things I did was send out an email to the department explaining that we would no longer prey on our community. If people deserved a ticket, I wanted them to get a ticket. If people deserved a warning, I wanted them to get a warning. I wanted our focus to be on showing up for the community. Instead of walking out the door thinking about how many tickets they needed to write, I wanted officers to think about how they could positively impact the community. If that was through traffic enforcement, that was fine, but if it was through other means, that was fine, too. Traffic enforcement is needed, but it shouldn't be the sole thing police departments focus on. Being in a position to effect organization-wide change was something I had aspired to do, and it was humbling to be able to do that.

When I took the chief job in Ferguson, the question that I got asked the most was, "Why on Earth would you take that job?" Just about everyone in policing knows what happened in Ferguson after Michael Brown was killed. For me, going to Ferguson wasn't about being in the spotlight; it was about getting an opportunity. I had been putting in the work to position myself to compete for a chief job, and now opportunity was knocking at the door. But this wasn't just any chief job; it was Ferguson. Ferguson is a monster unlike any other place, and I didn't know if I was capable of handling everything that came with such a notable and challenging job. My wife and I talked at length about the pros and cons of the position. She probably felt more comfortable about what I could accomplish there than I did at the time.

One conversation really helped put things in perspective for me and helped me understand the assignment I was about to embark on. The only person affiliated with Forest Park who knew I was actively seeking chief jobs was our chaplain, Dr. B. A few days after receiving my first ever letter to interview for a chief position, I saw Dr. B at the PD, and he shared something with me. Dr. B told me that he had had a vision, and God had shown him that I was a police chief. Dr. B said he had not seen where I was a police chief, but he'd seen it clear as day that I was a chief. I waited until I left work that day and then called Dr. B to tell him how timely his vision was because I had just been notified about the chief interview. He was sure to remind me that his vision did not reveal where I would be a chief, so I needed to stay grounded about the upcoming process.

While my wife and I were still pondering whether to take the Ferguson job or not, I ran into Dr. B. I told him about the offer to be the chief in Ferguson, but I was hesitant to accept because it was Ferguson. Dr. B reminded me that I had been seeking an opportunity like this, and I didn't get to question the one that God had put before me. His analogy was simple: "You've been asking God for an apple, and when he gives you an apple, you want to turn it down because it's a green apple instead of a red apple? It doesn't work like that. Why are we talking about this? You know what you need to do." He was right; I had to trust that my journey had prepared me for this moment, and now it was time to prove to myself that I belonged.

What gave me confidence that I could have success in Ferguson was how similar the community was to Forest Park. Both cities had a comparable population, the crime rates were similar, they were situated similarly geographically in their metro area, and they both had transitioned to majority-minority communities after historically being white communities. The approach was the same, but the stakes were a lot higher with Ferguson's history. I was hopeful that my commitment to showing up for the community would resonate with the people in Ferguson and fuel our progress.

Another area where I felt I was uniquely positioned to have an impact was my willingness to speak out when I saw something wrong within law enforcement. Many of the high-profile cases we had seen across the country had elements that I found problematic, and I didn't shy away from saying so. While I believe Sandra Bland died by suicide, the trooper who arrested her handled that situation all wrong, and it should not have escalated to her ending up in jail in the first place. Although there is no video of the shooting of Philando Castile, I believe the officer overreacted because he was overwhelmed by the situation, which should not have been the case.

I often get asked about the Michael Brown shooting. First, let me clarify that the Ferguson Police Department did not investigate that shooting, so I did not have access to the case file while I was there. With that said, I talked with a lot of people who played a part in reviewing or investigating the incident. As tragic as that event was, I cannot say it was an unjustified shooting. I'm aware of three different entities that independently investigated that incident, and none of them ruled it unjustified or an excessive use of force. My personal thoughts on that incident are that both individuals made poor decisions that contributed to how the situation played out. If there was a way to go back in time and relive that moment, I'm confident that Darren Wilson and Michael Brown would both make different decisions that day.

It's hard to navigate a conversation about the Brown shooting because people have such concrete feelings about what they think happened. With the "Hands up, don't shoot" narrative that spread after the shooting, many people strongly believe that Michael Brown surrendered before he was shot and killed. I don't believe Michael Brown was standing there with his hands in the air when he was fatally shot, but I do think it's possible that his hands were elevated at some point during the altercation. The federal investigation report lays out very clearly that eyewitnesses and physical evidence support that Michael Brown was coming toward Darren Wilson when he was shot and killed. Several witnesses from the neighborhood reported that he was "charging" at Darren Wilson. Despite the complexities of these incidents, law enforcement leaders have to be able to navigate these difficult conversations in a way that doesn't contribute to furthering the community divide.

When I arrived in Ferguson, I knew the significance of my words had elevated to a new level. Overnight, my name and picture were being circulated around the country, and I was thrust into the law enforcement spotlight. If I wasn't careful with my words, I could spark widespread resentment, fuel protests, or, even worse, ignite rioting. This is where my friendship with V really paid off. I learned the importance of speaking with empathy and compassion in conjunction with stating my professional stance on any given matter. While I can't say that Darren Wilson was unjustified for shooting Michael Brown, I can still say that my heart goes out to the Brown family because I can't imagine how devastating it must be to lose a child. As the father of a teenage son, I can't imagine that level of pain.

As I started to do more public speaking and more national media interviews, I tried to convey a balanced message. There is a duality that exists with all of us, and none of us are 100% one thing or another. While some members of law enforcement may have done some horrible things under their law enforcement authority, that doesn't erase the good things they did in service to their community. We are all complicated beings, and at any moment, we have the capacity for good just as we have the capacity for bad.

People often want to hear my take on situations from the perspective of a black police chief. As I found myself navigating these conversations more and more, it highlighted the responsibility I held of being viewed as a trusted voice. One thing that challenged me in this space was a social media group I was invited to join. It was a law enforcement group, and one of my colleagues had added me to it. I didn't think much about it at the time and accepted the invitation. I don't remember how long I was part of this group before I realized that it was not for me, but it wasn't very long. I don't recall what I saw in this group; I just remember that it didn't align with my views of society, so I left.

Some time went by, and another one of my colleagues added me to the group again. Not thinking much about it, I accepted the invitation. After joining the group the second time, it didn't take long for me to be reminded why I'd left it the first time. Someone in the group posted a news article about George Zimmerman auctioning off the gun with which he'd shot and killed Trayvon Martin. The caption was something like: "I hope he makes millions off of this." What transpired after that was comment after comment supporting the original post. People had nasty things to say about Trayvon Martin, and none of them had ever met this young man.

What this moment highlighted for me was the level of division in our society and the lack of decency that some people have. No matter your views on the Trayvon Martin situation, he didn't go looking for trouble with George Zimmerman that evening. Why is this young man being dragged through the mud for being killed? The comments were so bad that I started to type a rebuttal. As my comment got longer and longer, I realized that my words would not land how I wanted them to. I realized that initiating an argument with people I didn't know and would probably never meet was not the best use of my time and energy. So, I deleted the comment and simply left the group again. This time, I posted a statement on my page to my fellow law enforcement colleagues not to add me to that group again. I didn't fault them for being in the group; I simply explained that my values were not represented there and that it was best for me not to be in it.

Race is one of the biggest dividers in American society to this day, and it will probably always play an integral role in our nation's dynamics. While I identify as black, the truth of the matter is that I am biracial. My father is African-American, and my mother is Native American. Growing up, I didn't have a multi-race box to check; I had to check only one, so that box was always black for me. Growing up biracial is difficult because you don't fully belong to any group. Clearly, I was black, but I was light-skinned with green eyes, so I was different from my black family and friends. My given nickname in grade school was "Oreo." While I laughed it off publicly, inside I struggled with my identity.

While I did not have a tumultuous childhood, I do remember one terrible experience I had with racism. I was 13 or 14 at the time, and my parents bowled in a Friday night bowling league. Every Friday night, I was at the bowling alley with the same kids in the game room. The primary attractions there were the two pool tables. It cost 50 cents a game, and you placed your two quarters on the table ledge to signify that you had the next game.

Before this one night, it never really set in for me that I was usually the only black kid in the game room on Friday nights. That night, someone's 50 cents went missing from the ledge. The money belonged to a kid around my age, and he had an older brother who was around 18 or 19. As they were trying to figure out what had happened to the missing money, the older brother turned, pointed directly at me, and said, "It had to be him because he is the only one in here with brown fingers!" I immediately went on the defensive, denying the accusation, and then I left the game room to sit where my parents were bowling.

Several people from the game room came to check on me and apologize. They found out what had happened with the 50 cents, and it turned out to be a complete misunderstanding. After leaving the bowling alley that evening, I told my parents what had happened. The following

Friday, my father repeatedly came into the game room to check on me. The older brother never apologized to me; he just acted friendly toward me after that incident. I share this story often because we often only think of the N-word as the catalyst of hatred and racism. I've been called the N-word several times, but none of them have stung as much as this incident did.

Throughout my career, I have had to navigate many circumstances where race was inserted into the equation. On multiple occasions, while arresting a white person, I've been called the N-word. I've had to navigate personnel issues where an officer was accused of making a comment or reference to a racial slur, sometimes internally and sometimes externally. I had to keep my composure while taking a burglary report from a white family, and the small child (five or six) told me that he was sure the burglar was black. I've had to stand in the house of an elderly white lady before and listen to her go on about how all the blacks and Hispanics that were moving into her neighborhood were turning her neighborhood into a "black ghetto."

I say all this to show that how we address race matters, especially when we are talking about law enforcement. Do we allow space to have the conversations that need to be had, and do we have the right people navigating the discussion? One of the most frustrating parts of my career has been my accomplishments being validated because of my race. When I was an acting captain in Forest Park, I was having a conversation with a fellow officer who was a friend of mine. We started talking about the upcoming captain process, and he said to me, "You're black, and there has never been a black captain before. Of course, you are going to get promoted." He wasn't saying it to be disrespectful, and I realized the truth of the matter is that he was comfortable enough with me to say it to my face—and that others thought the same thing.

Naturally, my rebuttal was to spell out my resume and accomplishments to validate my case that I was the strongest candidate, period. I didn't have to deal with that as much when I arrived in Ferguson because the person I beat out for the job was black as well, but I did have to deal with it when I arrived in Apex. I came to Apex on the heels of public scrutiny after a cultural assessment report went public stating the department suffered from racial bias problems. Many assumed that hiring the first black police chief in the town's history was a consequence of the fallout.

I had been invited to attend a local community group's monthly meeting and introduce myself. During the Q&A portion of my introduction, one of the attendees asked me to explain my plans for the department because there were some concerns among community members over how I had been hired. This comment took me aback because I had no clue what she was inferring with her notion that I was hired for non-valid reasons. I felt that she was questioning my talents and abilities because she assumed the primary reason I had been hired was because I was black. I explained the hiring process that I had gone through, which included an assessment process facilitated by an outside executive search firm. Of course, I mentioned how I'd finished number one—by a sizable margin from what I'd heard—and was clearly the best candidate for what the town was looking for.

When I speak with fellow minorities in law enforcement, we often talk about feeling as though we have to work twice as hard and be twice as good to have a fair chance of succeeding or advancing. I imagine minorities in other professions feel the same way all too often. Part of my *why* is establishing myself as one of the greatest at my craft so that when people talk about me and my legacy, they talk about my accomplishments and leave it at that.

Whenever people meet me in person, the first thing that they usually comment on is my size. I stand at 6'5" and weigh roughly 245 lbs. I'm built like an athlete, so the natural conversation starter for most people is to ask me if I played football or basketball and where. While that is often an innocent question, it has motivated me for decades. I dislike the assumption that a physically imposing black male has to be connected to sports. No one has ever walked up to me and asked me if I was a doctor or a rocket scientist. I have channeled that motivation to push myself to be great at my craft and valuable for my knowledge, not my physical attributes.

While that is my example of what motivates me, the people in my community have their own historical experiences that contribute to how they want to show up in the world. The more we are intentional in recognizing and highlighting our differences, the better chance we have to be an inclusive community. I want to be a part of a community where everyone is lifted up for the value they bring. I want my kids to feel a sense of belonging in whatever community they choose. That is how we build strong communities. Building community is my *why*!

CHAPTER 6

THE REFORM

Reform is a very popular word in law enforcement these days. Critics cry out for more reforms, while law enforcement often pushes back against reforms we feel will make it unsafe for officers to do their jobs. Personally, I'm a fan of reform and have built my career as a chief on reform. For me, it is a lot simpler than all the fighting and bickering would have you believe.

The Merriam-Webster Dictionary defines reform as "to amend or improve by change of form or removal of faults or abuses." In its simplest form, reform means to improve. I think we all need to improve in every facet of our lives, so why would I be against reform?

My first reform effort was when I sent that email about our traffic enforcement culture in Forest Park. I wasn't trying to put an end to us making traffic stops; I just wanted us to have a better outlook on how we used them. In my opinion, by improving how we approached traffic stops, we could improve how the community perceived us. For me, reform work is simple. What are things that the community is complaining about, and how can we get creative in addressing their concerns?

I can't talk about reform and not talk about the work that we did in Ferguson. For those who are not aware, Ferguson is under a federal consent decree. A consent decree is an agreement between parties that spells out specific mandates that have to be met by the defendant in the case. How does a police department end up on a consent decree? The Department of Justice has a Civil Rights Division, and they conduct what's called "patterns or practice" investigations. If the DOJ determines a pattern or practice of unconstitutional policing is present within the police department under investigation, a consent decree is typically the result. Ferguson's consent decree contains 464 paragraphs, and each is basically a stipulation that the department has to comply with.

In 2024, Ferguson was a community of around 18,000 residents, and the police department had approximately 60 full-time staff members, including officers, dispatchers, and support staff. In comparison, Baltimore's consent decree contains 510 paragraphs, and New Orleans's consent decree contains 492 paragraphs. In 2024, Baltimore's population was around 575,000, and the police department had approximately 2,800 employees. New Orleans's population was around 350,000, and the police department had about 1,400 employees. While the consent decree documents for the three cities were similar in size, the resources available for reform work were vastly different.

When it comes to reform, the main focal point is often your organization's accountability system. Regardless of what type of organization you are in, especially if it's law enforcement, having a subpar accountability system will come back to haunt your organization. When I arrived in Ferguson, I was hoping to be able to take my time getting acclimated to the organization before I had to make a splash with a big decision or change in the organization. As fate would have it, my first week in the position presented me with some difficult decisions.

On my third day on the job, I received an email from one of the council members alerting me to two incidents that had happened that week involving our officers. The first incident happened on Monday, my first day on the job. In that incident, one of our officers was extremely unprofessional in how they handled a call. Their actions—specifically their choice of words—added to the tensions of the call instead of de-escalating them. I talked to the supervisor about this incident and asked what they thought of how the officer had handled the call, and they answered that they thought the officer had done a good job. At that moment, I realized how much work I had ahead of me because my outlook was totally different.

While the Monday incident was problematic, it wasn't a critical failure and was properly addressed with a stern explanation and documentation of our expectations. The second incident was very different. It happened on Wednesday, my third day on the job. Once again, an officer had been unprofessional in handling a situation, but this interaction was different. Not only were the actions unprofessional, but I did not feel they were legally supported, given the information available at the time. While I cannot go into details about the incident, what I can share is that the Constitution and laws give us our authority, when applied appropriately, to exercise control over people or things. When our actions are not supported by legal authority, we are in the wrong. As part of my inquiry, I looked into the officer's history and found that they had a very extensive history of problematic behavior—so much so that I questioned how they had not been terminated due to their prior actions. I launched an official internal affairs investigation into this officer, and that investigation resulted in their termination.

I did not set out to make an immediate splash of this magnitude when I first arrived in Ferguson. I was not looking to strike fear into the officers at the department. I was simply addressing the matters that had been brought to my attention and had no control over how quickly they came to me. What I did have control over was doing the right thing when they popped up on my radar.

One thing was clear to me early on: We needed to reset our expectations as an organization and reform how we conducted business. I have to admit I was surprised to find this behavior my first week on the job. Clearly, I was naive in assuming that, considering the microscope Ferguson was under, every officer's behavior with the public would be above reproach. Even sending the message early on that unprofessional behavior would not be tolerated under my leadership didn't prevent unfortunate things from happening. However, the key to reform is that although I can't guarantee something bad won't happen, I can guarantee that if it does happen and we find out about it, we are going to take the necessary steps to properly address it. Throughout my tenure as chief, I was steadfast in that approach.

My actions early on did not resonate with everyone, and months later, I was dealing with an even bigger problem. I was briefed by one of my commanders about a use-of-force incident that was going to be problematic for us. Once the review packet made it to me and I saw what had happened, I felt that the use of force was not only unwarranted but excessive and criminal. As a result of the officer's actions, they were terminated, and the case was referred to an outside agency for a criminal investigation. Ultimately, the officer was indicted on federal charges of assaulting the person in their custody.

While it is never ideal to be associated with the criminal behavior of one of your officers, being praised for not tolerating that type of behavior was a positive for us.

It sucks when your department is in the headlines for negative behavior. It impacts everyone in the organization, and no one wants to be affiliated with that. The only positive to come from this incident was the coverage of the Ferguson Police Department doing the right thing. We were praised by the federal officials who handled the indictment. While it is never ideal to be associated with the criminal behavior of one of your officers, being praised for not tolerating that type of behavior was a positive for us. That is what reform is all about. It's not about creating the perfect officer or police department. It's about getting better and improving the systems in place, so everyone has a chance at fairness.

Those examples do not represent what normally goes on in a police department. Those examples do not represent the great work that was being done by the men and women of the Ferguson Police Department. Although such incidents get all of the headlines and attention, the day-to-day areas of improvement are what really drive reform work. Whenever law enforcement is dominating the headlines for something negative, one of the main talking points is that there is no national standard to follow. This is true; every state has its own requirements for law enforcement. There are several law enforcement associations, all of which produce best practices, but even those are not consistent.

The primary entity for the consistency of law enforcement practices is the Commission on Accreditation for Law Enforcement Agencies (CALEA). Many agencies strive to be CALEA certified, but CALEA takes a significant investment of staff time and financial support. Most agencies in the country are classified as small agencies and do not have the resources to do the CALEA process. I've had the luxury of working for a CALEA-accredited agency in Forest Park. In coming to Ferguson, I thought my experience with CALEA would aid me in the work of reforming the department under the consent decree. I was severely mistaken in that assumption; navigating a consent decree is very different from the CALEA process. In the reform work that we did in Ferguson, my goal was not to focus on the words of a document but on what the community was calling for. Since my focus was on the community, I needed a person whose primary focus was the words on the consent decree, and we lucked out when we landed Nicolle Barton as our new Consent Decree Coordinator.

Nicolle came to us with a background in civilian oversight of law enforcement. Before meeting her, I had never heard of the National Association for Civilian Oversight of Law Enforcement (NACOLE). What I learned from her is that there is an entire network of oversight practitioners committed to changing the policing profession.

Now, I have to admit, as a career police officer, my first notion about NACOLE was that someone who has never done the job of a police officer could not possibly tell us how to do it best. I'm sure I speak for most law enforcement when I say that. There are plenty of people who hold an opinion on what or how we should do things but don't dare to walk into the spaces we run into.

Nicolle was the first person responsible for leading consent decree efforts in Ferguson who was not a sworn law enforcement official. I can't say that I would have decided to bring in a civilian to manage our consent decree efforts. The decision to go that route had been made before I arrived in Ferguson. Nicolle did not report to me; we both reported to the town manager, so we were equals.

The two of us did amazing work together, and we moved the needle on reform efforts. Nicolle's most significant contribution was with community impact. She emphasized community while I advocated for officers, and together, we found a balance. I helped Nicolle argue our side when it came to conflicts with the DOJ, and she helped me argue the community impact side when it came to conflicts with officers. Balance was what I was looking for, and it helped to have someone with a different perspective. While we did not see eye to eye on a lot of things, we both had the same goal in mind.

Nothing put our reform efforts to the test like Ferguson's Civilian Review Board (CRB). The CRB was made up of community members tasked with reviewing complaint investigations and rendering a finding for me to take into consideration before making a final decision. Before I arrived in Ferguson, the CRB had not received these investigation reports, but I made it a priority to get the ball rolling on this part of the process. I'm happy to say that in the majority of investigations they reviewed, they had the same findings as the department. But the handful of cases where they had a different opinion than the department did were like heavyweight boxing matches.

That's another place where Nicolle really shined. She understood our process and how the findings were applied. She was our liaison to the CRB, so she worked with them to help them understand processes and the elements of findings. A quick example of this is if a dispatcher is rude or unprofessional with someone on the phone. The phone lines are recorded, so it was pretty easy to determine what had happened. While we could confirm that the behavior was inappropriate, that did not mean that the dispatcher would be terminated. If the action was not egregious or detrimental and the employee did not have any previous history of this behavior, progressive discipline was appropriate.

On multiple occasions, however, the CRB wanted the employee terminated for minor infractions. On other occasions, the CRB wanted to sustain the claims against the employee when there was no evidence to support it. In instances when we can not confirm or deny a claim against an employee, the claim is often ruled "not sustained." It doesn't exonerate the employee; it just means there is not enough information available to render a finding in favor of or against the employee. The CRB struggled with these cases because they often made their decision based on the allegation, regardless of the fact that there was no evidence to support it. If the allegation sounded bad, which most do, they wanted action taken against the employee.

While the CRB took up a lot of our time and energy, we were committed to our reform work with the broader community. Nothing drove the reform discussion more than the deaths of George Floyd and Breonna Taylor. One positive of being under a consent decree is that we had already undergone just about all the changes to policy that the country was calling for. That still did not keep Ferguson's name out of the national media spotlight, and we were regularly referenced in interviews or commentary. That resulted in a lot of media interviews with me talking about what the president said or what some congressperson said about the state of affairs of policing. I used the media coverage to highlight the good work being done in Ferguson. Locally, we had received praise for how we'd handled the riots after George Floyd. That gave us a platform to discuss changes we had made as an organization and how we were leading the country in reform efforts.

One of our biggest reform efforts was increasing the community input that went into our policies and procedures. All the policies related to our consent decree and reform efforts were published for public comment prior to being finalized. The DOJ would receive that input and insert it into the policy for another round of internal review. We even partnered with the Ferguson-Florissant School District on a policy review that primarily impacted teens. The policy was sent to high school seniors for their input, and we received a great deal of feedback from them. We were actually surprised that so many of them participated, but it showed that when you give people a chance to be involved, they may just surprise you.

Reform must be rooted in what is best for the community and with an emphasis on sustainability. The unfortunate reality is that politics often hijack sound thinking, and knee-jerk decisions are made. This was magnified with the "defund" movement. I have not met a police chief in the country who has said that they have all the resources they need to provide the highest quality of service to their community. With that being the reality of law enforcement, how could anyone think taking away the resources that they do have would help improve things?

When the commentary first started about police funding, I don't believe the intent was to defund the police. People were advocating for resources for community support, which I feel most law enforcement agrees with. The more community support and resources there are, the less the police get called to handle situations that are better suited for professional practitioners. I think everyone would like to see that happen, but that will only be successful with funding of those resources, not taking funding away from law enforcement.

Despite how much we may want to remove officers from responding to certain calls, there is always going to be a need for them to be involved in many of them. A double homicide in my community highlighted this notion. The original call that came in was for an individual who was believed to be experiencing a mental health crisis. Two neighbors went to check on him because he was outside, acting erratically. Unfortunately, the individual was armed with a gun, and he shot and killed his two neighbors. Thankfully, officers had been dispatched, and they were close by when the call changed to a shooting incident. They arrived quickly to take the shooter into custody before anyone else was harmed.

One of the training courses I teach focuses on the transition from protest to policy and the steps that need to be in place to get to a place of stability. A big part of that work is how partnerships are formed in the community and how we get the right people involved in the work that has to be done. Most people are familiar with the saying, "How do you eat an elephant? One bite at a time." That's how you tackle the reform efforts you are experiencing, especially if you have experienced a crisis.

Law enforcement often pushes back against reform changes when they feel they are already doing the things that people are calling for. I was asked to consult a police department that was dealing with the aftermath of a critical incident. One of their officers had shot and killed an unarmed person while trying to take them into custody. The incident had racial undertones as the victim was a minority and the officer was white. The police chief left shortly after the incident happened, and an internal interim chief was leading during the crisis.

When an incident like this happens, the local elected officials normally get involved with community members to try and plan what reform is going to look like to prevent it from happening again. While it's important to work with the community on what the future holds, police leadership needs to have a seat at the table. As I talked with the leadership team at this department, they shared the challenges they were facing and how their department had been falsely portrayed negatively. They felt they didn't have any support from their local government and the world was against them. When we talked about the things that were happening and what was being offered for them to change or implement, they argued that they already had those things in place or they were already doing those things.

Here's the thing: When your agency is involved in an incident that makes national headlines, get prepared for change. But change doesn't have to be a big fight. My advice in this situation is simple:

1. Listen to what people are saying they want to see from you.
2. Review your policies to see what changes are appropriate.
3. Ask for input from community stakeholders.
4. Learn from those who have been in that situation previously.

Simply arguing that you already do the things that are being asked of you is not going to work. When people demand change, you have to be intentional about looking for ways for them to be heard so they feel like their concerns are being taken seriously.

Another strategy I see departments get wrong is making enemies of the people who are newly involved. After a critical incident, especially one that involves questionable police action, people in the community feel a need to get involved. Unfortunately, too often, it takes a crisis for this to happen, but you will have a new segment of people to deal with. It's understandable to be turned off by people popping up only after a critical incident. However, you need to be focused on finding partners for you and the organization, not giving people more reasons not to like you or your organization. This is the time for you to gauge who is showing up because they care about the community and want to contribute to things getting better and who is showing up because they want some air time or notoriety.

I had to learn this lesson the hard way. When I went to Ferguson, I was under the impression that all activists and "loud" people wanted things to get better for the community. I soon learned that not everyone wanted the relationship between the police and the community to get better. Some people wanted things to remain contentious so they could maintain their relevance as adversaries of the police.

That was disheartening to see, but I had to roll with it. You learn over time who these individuals are and that you cannot invest too much of your time and energy into them; instead, you invest in the people who are genuinely trying to help bring positive change. I would still engage with these individuals and maintain an open avenue of communication, but I didn't let it dominate my time and energy because their intentions were clearly self-serving. People who are newly engaged after the incident can become a great resource and partners for what you are trying to accomplish. Don't be so turned off by their motivation that you lose out on a great connection.

Reform work is hard, and leading reform work is even harder. What I've learned on this journey is that it is extremely difficult to help people understand your vision. One reason for this is that people bring their hurt and frustration to the discussion, and sometimes, human nature won't let us see past our own feelings.

As I mentioned earlier, before I arrived at Apex, the department had been in the headlines for a cultural assessment report that said the department had a culture of racial bias. Prior to these findings going public, the department had taken another hit in the media for a dispute involving one of the officers and their neighbor over a Christmas card. By the time I arrived in Apex, a group of community members had formed an advocacy group to advocate for accountability of the police department. This group asked for regular meetings with me to learn what changes had been implemented within the department since my arrival. After seeing what we were doing as an organization, this group became comfortable with the department and the reform work we were doing. Because this group was willing to engage, they had the benefit of learning what we were trying to accomplish as an organization, and they agreed with the direction we were headed in.

While it was an accomplishment to build that trust with the group, I lost some of the department's trust as a result. Some of my staff felt that I was catering to this group and cared more about what they wanted to see. That wasn't the case, and there were plenty of things that the group wanted to see from me or the department that I would not do, but I was willing to engage and be open with them, and they appreciated that. I understand why some of my staff felt the way that they did, but doing this work has taught me that you have to be willing to do what may not be the most beneficial for you personally when you know it's the right thing to do.

One tactic that I use to build trust is to give people an opportunity to be a part of important processes so they can see firsthand what goes on behind the scenes. This tactic can be used internally and externally. When I came to Apex, I created a new non-sworn (civilian) position that would be in charge of our office of professional standards. To highlight my commitment to bringing people in, I had one of the members from the accountability community group serve as an assessor for the hiring process for this position. I have to give another shout-out to Nicolle Barton for this. Basically, I took her consent decree role and made it an executive-level position within the police department. This position would oversee citizen complaints and internal affairs investigations and would touch all liability areas, such as use-of-force and pursuit reviews. This position was the equivalent of a sworn police captain with the same authority.

Once again, this was not a popular decision in the organization. Police officers inherently do not feel comfortable having their actions critiqued by civilians who have never done the job. Some officers felt I had created this position to hunt for mistakes so I could discipline and terminate officers. That couldn't have been further from the truth.

I had two primary reasons for creating this civilian position. First, we regularly heard from community members that they didn't trust the police to investigate their own and hold them accountable. Having civilian oversight, especially when that civilian has never been a police officer, adds credibility to the integrity of the investigation. While I understand that some officers don't like that stance, it's an added layer of protection for them to promote confidence in investigations.

Second, when writing reports, officers naturally fill in the blanks with their experience, and that is not always fair to the public. I'm also speaking about myself when I make that statement. After years of doing this job, you become conditioned to certain actions, meaning certain things, especially when it comes to defiance. A quick example of this is a supervisor investigating a minor citizen complaint. After the citizen files the initial complaint, it's not uncommon to not be able to get back in touch with them despite calling several times. When the report is turned in, it will often read something like this: "I called the complainant multiple times, and they refused to answer my calls." In my professional opinion, using the word "refused" puts an unfair label on the complainant. Using that word suggests that the complainant is intentionally avoiding talking to us and could leave the impression that they have something to hide or are being untruthful in their claims. The only facts are that the person did not answer our calls or call us back. That's all the paperwork should say: nothing more, nothing less.

At the end of the day, it's our quality of service to the community that should be at the forefront of what we do.

Throughout the years, I have repeatedly seen officers use wording like this that slant things in their favor. When I see reports from a civilian practitioner, they are usually more evenly balanced. I'm not saying that a sworn officer can't do a good job of investigating and holding another officer accountable; I just feel the community gets a better product when civilian practitioners are part of the process. At the end of the day, it's our quality of service to the community that should be at the forefront of what we do.

Many organizations need to undergo internal reform. What are the things that you can do to get better as an organization? This is more complicated than it sounds, or at least it has been more complicated for me on my journey. I once started a group in the police department called the Chief's CIRCLE. CIRCLE stands for Communication, Innovation, Responsibility, Commitment, Leadership, and Empowerment. To be eligible, you had to be below the rank of a command-level position, so front-line supervisors and non-supervisors were the only people in the group. My reason for this was that command-level staff members had regular access to me through command staff meetings, executive staff meetings, and the normal flow of business, or so I thought.

One of the biggest complaints in police departments is the different treatment of sworn staff compared to civilian staff. I intentionally made sure I had civilian representation in the Chief's CIRCLE so they could equally contribute to the discussions that impacted the organization. The purpose of this group was to provide an arena where line staff had direct access to me to talk about the things they felt didn't properly filter down to their level. They could hear my comments on matters, and I would discuss initiatives with this group that impacted the entire department. Sounds like a good way to get buy-in from people, right?

The Chief's CIRCLE was not at all as successful as I had hoped. Some of my command-level folks felt that line staff got information before they received it, so that was problematic for them. Some things talked about in the Chief's CIRCLE were shared outside the agency and that contributed to people being misinformed about things I was trying to do. In all, it wasn't a success, but we tried something new, and that is half the battle when it comes to reform.

Placing a civilian executive over professional standards was not a popular decision, but it was something new. That change was a great success for us, and I talk about our program when I speak around the country because I think other departments and communities can benefit from implementing a similar approach.

Another important internal component to look at is who is restricted from joining your department. That may sound weird, but hear me out. The law enforcement profession is a very different place now than when I first started. I often challenge agencies to look at their appearance policy and then go around the community and identify people who could not work for them because of what it restricts. Beards and tattoos have come a long way in terms of how they are accepted in the profession, but there are still a lot of things that need to be taken into consideration: What hairstyles are allowed? Can males wear earrings? Can officers wear the same nail polish colors as civilian staff who do not leave the building? Can male officers wear nail polish? How welcoming are we to people who are looking to enter the profession? When we talk about reform, we have to be open to where it may lead us. It may not be to where we initially thought, but if we end up in a better place than when we started, I count that as success.

CHAPTER 7

THE LESSONS

I have learned many lessons throughout my career, and they have shaped me both professionally and personally. These lessons are a big part of why I am the person I am today. One of the best compliments I have received as police chief is that I am authentic. I'm going to be me whether it is to my benefit or detriment. I have prided myself on this. I feel obliged to share my truth on any matter being discussed. As you can imagine, that does not always pan out the best for me, but hey, I don't know how to be any other way.

I want to begin this chapter by talking about people. I've had an amazing career spanning more than two decades in three cities in three different states, and I was honored to sit in the chief's seat at each stop. What I have learned during this journey is that there is little difference in what you are going to get from people, no matter where you are or what you are doing. My favorite phrase is, "People are people."

I saw a visual one time, and it has become a go-to for explaining the leadership journey to up-and-coming leaders. If you will indulge me, I have a simple exercise for you to do. Take out a piece of paper or use a technical device to draw a triangle that is pointed up. Now, draw two additional horizontal lines inside the triangle. These two lines should be evenly spaced apart from the tip of the triangle down to the base. What you should see is that the bottom line of the triangle is the longest, the next line up is shorter because it goes from sideline to sideline, the next line up is even shorter, and then you have the tip where the two sidelines come together at the top. Essentially, you have created a small triangle, a medium triangle, and a large triangle.

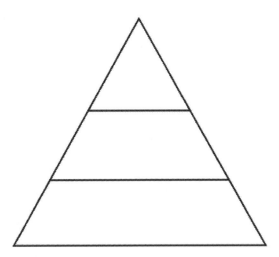

At the bottom-left corner of the large triangle, write "90%." At the bottom-left corner of the medium triangle, write "70%." At the bottom-left corner of the small triangle, write "30%," and to the left of the tip of the large triangle, write "10%." At the bottom-right corner of the large triangle, write "10%." At the bottom-right corner of the medium triangle, write "30%." At the bottom-right corner of the small triangle, write "70%," and to the right of the tip of the large triangle, write "90%." To ensure you did it correctly, each line across should equal 100%.

Now, under the "90%" at the bottom-left corner, write "Technical Skills," and under the "10%" at the bottom-right corner, write "People Skills." Your drawing should look like the following image. What you are looking at are the skills you will need as you climb the leadership ladder.

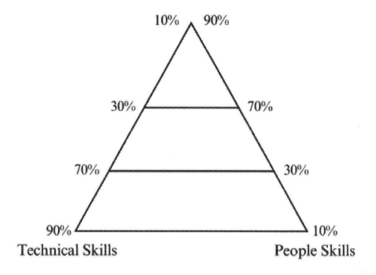

At the bottom, it is more about your technical knowledge, skills, and abilities, but as you climb, it becomes less and less about your technical skills and more about your people skills. Just because you are great at doing the job, it does not mean you will be great at leading people as they do the job. Sports is a great example of this. Some of the greatest coaches in professional sports never played professional sports. Or, if they did play, they were not stars but were mediocre at best. On the other hand, we have seen some stars try their hand at coaching, and they are often not very successful. Why is that? Look at your drawing. There is your answer.

I can't think of a better example to highlight my triangle example than my experience as a newly promoted sergeant. I had been a sergeant for less than a month before I found myself getting written up for not properly handling a situation. At the beginning of a patrol shift, you have a roll call (team briefing). That's when the watch commander goes over important information for the shift. On this particular day, Officer T, a female officer assigned to a different unit, came into roll call. It was not uncommon for someone from another unit to attend roll call. While in the room, Officer T made some vague comments aloud, but clearly, they were about someone specific. I didn't know what she was referring to, so I paid little attention to it.

Later on in the day, a female officer on my team, Officer M, came to me and complained that Officer T was being rude and disrespectful toward her. She stated that Officer T had been looking at her when she'd made her comments during roll call. Officer M explained to me the history between the two of them, and after hearing that, the comments now made sense to me. I told her I would talk to Officer T and squash all the drama. I sought out Officer T, told her that I'd heard what she said, and explained that I felt she'd been directing her comments at Officer M. Then I essentially instructed her to knock off the crap. That was pretty much it from me, short and sweet. I felt this situation was childish. Both of these women were mothers and older than me, and they were better off directing their energy elsewhere.

Well, it turned out the drama was very significant to Officer T. She filed a grievance against Officer M and a complaint against me. Her complaint was that I did not take the matter seriously and that it felt like I didn't care. She was right! When my supervisor gave me my write-up, I couldn't argue against that claim because it was accurate. I viewed the situation as a waste of my time.

The lesson I learned is that it doesn't matter what I think of a situation; my job as the leader is to make it better, not worse. Another lesson I learned from this is that friendship does not trump your responsibilities in leadership. Officer T was a friend of mine. That made me think I could have an informal, matter-of-fact conversation with her instead of the formal supervisor conversation that I should have had.

I'm pretty sure most of us have vivid memories of times when we felt severely wronged by someone or something. I don't know if this woman is still around or not, but there is an elderly female that I owe an apology to. I mentioned several times now how traffic stops and tickets were our primary focus at my first agency. It was not acceptable to come in at the end of the shift with no tickets unless a crisis had taken up your entire shift.

One evening, while I was in field training, it had gotten late into the shift, and my training officer and I hadn't written any tickets yet. My training officer was not certified to issue speeding tickets, so we could not operate the radar device. So, in the wee hours of the morning, we would set up in a residential neighborhood to watch a stop sign. I was driving, and I'm pretty sure my field training officer had fallen asleep in the passenger seat by this point.

After a while, I saw a vehicle fail to come to a complete stop, and I pulled out to make the traffic stop. There were no other cars on the road, just us and this vehicle. When I got to the driver's door, I discovered the driver was a black female in her 50s. She was not rude to me and hadn't "blown through" the stop sign; she just hadn't come to a complete stop. Despite this, my training officer instructed me to issue her a citation, largely because we hadn't written any tickets yet.

I will never forget what she said to me when I explained to her that she was being issued a ticket: "Why are you doing this? You know this is wrong. I don't deserve this ticket." She was right! Her actions were minor, and they had not impacted anyone. She deserved to get a warning, but because I had no voice in the matter, she received a ticket. I wish I had taken her name down. I would love nothing more than to be able to send her an apology for giving her that ticket and explain to her that her words helped me see that people shouldn't be treated like stats but as people. The lesson I learned from this encounter is that decisions that impact others should be grounded in fairness, not survival. I should have fought for that lady because it was fair for her to get a warning and for us to get chewed out for not writing any tickets that shift.

In Chapter 1, I mentioned an experience with the N-word being uttered in a room full of people. I was a captain in Forest Park at the time, and I was still the only minority on the command staff. I was conducting roll call one day and briefing the team about a community event being held that day. The event was called Rosetown Day, and it was an annual community get-together held in the Rosetown neighborhood. When I mentioned the event, one of my newer officers, a black female, asked me what it entailed. After I explained the gist of it, she said, "Oh, it's like Ni**a Day!"

Of all the things that could have followed my explanation of Rosetown Day, that was the last thing I expected to hear. It was like all the air had been sucked out of the room. The group was a mix of black, white, and Hispanic officers. I don't remember my follow-up comment exactly, but it was something along the lines of, "I have no idea what that is, but it's not Rosetown Day, so we are just going to call this Rosetown Day." I ended roll call as quickly as I could because the comment completely sidetracked me.

As soon as I dismissed everyone, I called the officer aside and chewed her out for such an unprofessional comment. She explained that she had been referring to an actual community event held in Atlanta with that name. I explained that I didn't give a damn what she was referring to and that her comment was completely inappropriate and unprofessional. After our conversation, I could tell by the look on her face that she got my message and understood how problematic her comment was. I told her that I would report this to the major, and we would see what her official discipline was going to be.

Once I was done lashing out, I did some research online and discovered that there was a community event that had an official name (I can't recall what it was) but had become known as "Ni**a Day." After learning that, I felt confident that the officer was not trying to be derogatory in any way; she just had a serious lapse in judgment with her poor choice of words. While discipline was absolutely appropriate in this situation, I was hoping the department wouldn't advocate for terminating her for this because I didn't feel it was warranted.

This incident happened on a Saturday; the next day, in roll call, the officer apologized to her teammates for her inappropriate comment. On Monday, the executive staff was back at work, and I had to brief the major on what had happened. He immediately stated that she needed to be terminated. I had feared that this would be his response. I explained that I disagreed and didn't support termination. I explained that I'd researched the event and had documented proof that she had been referring to a real thing and had not intended to be derogatory in any way.

This incident reminded me of the one that had happened in the police corps. There was no racist intent on her behalf, but just the word coming out of her mouth was serious enough to warrant this discussion. The major went on to explain to me that the department had previously dealt with an issue where a black officer accused a white officer of using the N-word. There was no proof that it had happened, but the department had committed to terminating anyone who used the word. I understood where the major was coming from. Although I wasn't familiar with the previous incident, I still did not support terminating the officer in this instance.

After our discussion, we moved up to the assistant chief. Once I had explained everything to him, his reaction was the same as the major's. He also referred to the previous incident and said they had committed to termination if someone used the word. I explained to them the cultural differences of growing up in the black community where the word is often used in everyday dialogue versus when the word is used to denigrate a black person—as well as how some in the black community differentiate the meaning of the word with an "a" at the end as opposed to "er." I felt that the two of them understood my points and even agreed with me slightly, but they were locked into this decision because of the previous incident.

Next, we moved to the chief's office to meet with him. At this point, I was well-versed in the events and their aftermath. After I explained everything to the chief, he asked me what we needed from him. I explained that the three of us were not on the same page as to how to move forward. I supported going through our discipline process, while the major and assistant chief supported termination. I was relieved to hear from the chief that he did not support termination in this case. Because I'd immediately spoken to the officer about the improper language and confirmed that it was a real event, he felt that was an appropriate response. In the end, the incident was handled through our progressive discipline system, with the understanding that there would be zero tolerance for further missteps of this nature from the officer.

Walking out of the chief's office, I felt grateful. I was not appreciative that the chief sided with my decision; I was appreciative that I was the captain who had been dealt this situation. Being the only black person on the command staff, I don't know if my counterparts could have dealt with this situation like I had, given my history and life experience.

The lesson I learned from this situation was the value of diversity and representation. The question that I've wrestled with is, if this officer had been white, would I have had the same outlook and approach? If everything was the same and I truly felt the word came out of the person's mouth the same way it had come out of hers and there was no history with the individual that gave me concern or pause about racism, I'm pretty confident my defense of them would have been the same. Fortunately, I have not been put in that situation to find out.

Over the last several years, we have learned a great deal about trauma, including the ways that trauma manifests in our thoughts and bodies. Two experiences come to mind that highlight the impact of trauma for me. The first occurred during the #MeToo movement. I was still in Forest Park at the time. Late one evening, while I was in the office, a female student from

Howard University called to report an incident that had happened several months earlier. She explained that she had been hanging out in Atlanta with some friends and had left the party with a male associate. He brought her back to a location in Forest Park, where he made sexual advances on her. She declined to engage, but he persisted several times. At one point, he fondled her in a sensitive area of her body as she continued to deny his advances. Finally, she got fed up with the situation and left. Now she was calling to report the fondling.

As we were talking, I didn't understand why she was calling to report this months later. I knew there was little that could be done about this case, as there was no evidence of what had happened. We could talk to him, and he would probably confirm the encounter and say that he thought she was okay with his advances because she left the party with him so they could be alone. I was going through the motions, asking my questions, and then it finally hit me. She finally felt empowered to call and tell her story because of what was going on in the country with the #MeToo movement.

Once I realized that, my outlook on our conversation changed. I went from trying to understand why she was calling after all this time to making sure she felt heard and that my voice conveyed compassion. By the end of the call, we were laughing and talking junk to one another about our HBCU schools. The call ended well, but I was disappointed in myself for needing that revelation before giving all that I had to give to that conversation. I realized that I had been conditioned to get the information as quickly as possible and decipher if there was anything of value that I had to work with—and if there wasn't, I needed to get it over with so I could go on to the next thing.

> *What I have found is that giving my time to people who are struggling with trauma is a great way to show compassion. People often just want to feel heard, even if you can't help them with their problems.*

As a leader, one of the best traits you can have is compassion. One of the challenges of being a public figure in a leadership position is that, sometimes, opposing sides want your compassion to swing in their direction. What I have found is that giving my time to people who are struggling with trauma is a great way to show compassion. People often just want to feel heard, even if you can't help them with their problems.

One of the saddest things I've ever witnessed in my life is what a mother experienced in Ferguson over a six-month period. The nightmare started when her younger son was shot and killed by her older son. The mother and her daughter were at the residence when the shooting took place. About five months later, I received a call late one night that we had just had a murder. I responded to the shooting and learned that a 22-year-old male had been gunned down in the front yard after leaving the residence. After speaking with my team at the scene, I also learned that the victim was the older brother who had shot and killed his younger brother months earlier. Before leaving the scene, I saw the mother on the front porch with the rest of her family.

The next day, I received an update that the grandmother had gone into cardiac arrest and passed away after I'd left. To recap, this mother lost her youngest son, who was shot and killed by her oldest son. Then, months later, her oldest son was shot and killed in the front yard of her mother's home where they were staying, and later that same night, her mother died of a heart attack. I have no doubt that her mother died of a broken heart after losing both her grandsons to gun violence in such a short period.

A few months after the oldest son was killed, the mother showed up at the police department, wanting to speak with me. She was upset that we had not charged the suspect in her son's murder. The family believed that one of the younger son's friends was the one who had killed the older son. We did not have enough evidence to charge the suspect, largely because we could not locate him for an interview. The mother wanted me to go with her so she could show me where she believed the suspect lived. She had shown up unannounced, but I felt she needed my compassion at that moment, so I cleared my schedule to spend whatever time she needed me to. In the end, we still did not gain enough traction on the suspect to bring charges, but I feel the mother had comfort knowing that her son's case was important to us—and, in particular, important to me. Fortunately, not everything is as traumatic as that situation, but my heart still hurts for that mother for what she went through. I still hold out hope that she gets closure one day.

In Ferguson, one of the initiatives we started was to set up small group dialogue sessions. This was an opportunity for community members to engage with law enforcement, seek understanding, and foster better relationships. This initiative was primarily focused on police-community engagement. We had a mediation consultant facilitate the discussions. For our first session, we handpicked people from various parts of the community whom we felt confident could contribute to a healthy dialogue. I didn't want the first session to erupt in chaos because I feared it would not be easy to get people back to the table. I participated in this first session as well so I could experience it for myself before I brought my officers into this space.

One question asked by the facilitator changed my outlook on the possibilities of these dialogue sessions: "What keeps you up at night?" As we went around the room answering the question, the discussion took an unexpected turn when one of the community members started engaging with another about their response. For those not familiar, Ferguson is a small city, approximately six square miles. So, wherever you are in the city, you are not far away from another part. But when one community member explained what kept them up at night, it was a shock to one of the other community members because they did not experience the same problems in their neighborhood, which was only about a mile and a half away.

What was unique about this was that, as the police chief, I visited all the neighborhoods and spoke with community members about their challenges. Everyone wanted more police presence, but due to our limited resources, I had to prioritize how we deployed our officers. That was rarely an acceptable answer to a community member, especially if they had been the victim of a crime. Some crimes take priority over others, and that is just the fact of the matter. I would regularly get scolded by community members because they felt we didn't care about their concerns. However, in the dialogue session, when community members heard from their fellow community members about the challenges of their neighborhood, the information landed differently than when I talked about it. There was more compassion in the room when it was neighbor to neighbor instead of the police trying to explain the community's challenges. The lesson for me was that community-community dialogue helps with police-community dialogue.

The biggest lesson for me throughout the years was realizing the value that I add to the spaces that I am in. I don't mean for that to come off as arrogant or conceited, but where I have had the most impact is in spaces that I didn't feel comfortable in.

I recall being in a meeting with other area chiefs. There were maybe 20 to 25 chiefs in this meeting, but only two or three of us were black. I was the newest and youngest chief in the group. The group was talking about putting out a statement after a national law enforcement critical incident. The discussion was not going in a direction that I felt was conducive to the outcome that the group was seeking. The incident had a racial component to it, and I didn't think the message being crafted would resonate with the audience that we needed to reach. I waited to comment because I was hoping one of the other minorities felt the same way and would speak up about the concern. Because I was new to this group, I didn't think my comments would resonate with the others. When no one spoke up, I interjected and raised my concerns with the messaging that had been discussed. Ultimately, the group chose to go with the original messaging.

After the meeting, one of the other minority chiefs reached out to me and thanked me for raising my concerns. I learned then that there's power in being brave enough to say what others are uncomfortable saying. It may bring some heat your way, but if you are coming from a genuine place and have positive intentions with your actions, you will be okay. That is how I built such effective relationships with community members throughout the years. I would speak my truth about the shortcomings of my profession, and people were not used to someone being that honest with them. I think law enforcement is the greatest profession in the world, but we are far from perfect, and it is okay to say that. Sometimes, it's not enough to say that we have a few bad apples; sometimes, we need to show how we are hunting for those bad apples and removing them from the profession.

One of my greatest career accomplishments was being selected into the inaugural cohort of the Obama Foundation's USA Leaders Program. Seeing President Obama make history as the first black president gave me the confidence that I could accomplish similar feats in my profession. The program selected one hundred individuals from a wide range of professional areas to go through a six-month leadership program. The entire program was virtual, with the exception of a three-day in-person convening midway through.

When the list of the program participants came out, I read everyone's bios and found myself thinking that I was completely out of place with this group. There was only one other law enforcement professional. A lot of my cohorts worked in activism, organizing, and advocacy, and the bulk of my experience with such people was them expressing their discontent with law enforcement. Despite feeling out of place, I was excited about the opportunity.

The in-person convening was the highlight of the program. It was amazing to see people in person whom I had been engaging with for months in virtual meetings. One of my fondest experiences at the convening was when one of my cohorts came up to me and told me that they were looking forward to meeting and connecting with me the most because I was a police chief. This person did not have a very favorable view of the police.

My cohort told me that they wanted to talk with me because we were on opposite sides of the police-community dynamic, and they were interested in hearing my stance on some issues. My response to them was, "How do you know we are on opposite sides?" We went on to have a great conversation and learned that we had several things in common when it came to law enforcement actions and behavior. My cohort was very appreciative of our conversation, and it was eye-opening for them to learn that there were law enforcement officials like me.

I would go on to have several conversations with other members, and their comments were much the same. Many of them had never had an intimate conversation with a police official before, and they were surprised to hear how I spoke of community and to learn some of the things I was doing in the profession to help improve relationships and build bridges.

> *These are the little victories that are out there when we are willing to step outside of our comfort zone and show up in the spaces where we can have the biggest impact.*

Another favorite moment of mine was when one of my cohorts was comfortable enough with me to tell me that when he looked through the list of members and saw that a police chief had been selected for the program, he'd exclaimed, "Why in the world is a police chief in our group?" I was happy to break through a lot of the perceptions that some of my cohorts had about law enforcement. One of them told me that after our time together, he'd decided that maybe everyone who carries a gun for a living isn't so bad. These are the little victories that are out there when we are willing to step outside of our comfort zone and show up in the spaces where we can have a positive impact.

Throughout my law enforcement journey, my greatest lesson has been the importance of family. My family has sacrificed a tremendous amount for me to have the career that I've had. Many days, I'd come home after seeing some horrible things and just want to be alone and not talk to anyone. I didn't want to go anywhere or do things because it was too hard to muster up the mental fortitude to be around people and engage with them. These are the things that people don't realize come with the crown of leadership. You carry the burdens of whatever group you lead, but who carries your burdens? Often, if you're lucky, it's your family and friends. I could not have been more blessed to have the support system of loved ones that I have in my life.

One day, as the chief in Ferguson, I was at home in my "man cave," alone, and I started thinking about something. I don't even remember what I was thinking about, but whatever it was, it caused me to start crying. My five-year-old daughter just happened to come upstairs. She asked me what was wrong, and I said, "I don't know." Like any five-year-old faced with a dilemma involving Daddy, she went and got Mommy. When my wife came to check on me, she, too, asked me what was wrong, but I couldn't really explain why I was so emotional; I just was. At that moment, they just loved on me. I wasn't being weak, and I wasn't less of a husband or a father; I was just a person having an emotional moment, and I had loved ones there to support me through it.

Knowing that I have that level of support is everything. It has taught me to dream even bigger and be bold—so bold that while writing this book, I announced my plans to retire early from policing. As long as I serve as a police chief, my commitment and energy have to be focused on that community. I feel very strongly that the lessons I have learned throughout my career can help communities not just across the United States but across the world. So, I chose to go all in on my consulting business, Armstrong Consulting, LLC, to have a bigger impact on the profession and communities that want to see better from law enforcement. If there is one thing that has been consistent about all the lessons throughout the journey, it is that I have accomplished everything I have set out to do, so why should I think any differently about my future endeavors?

CHAPTER 8

THE RESULTS

All that I have poured into my career is highlighted by the results that I have seen at every stop along the way. Through my journey, I have developed an unwavering confidence in myself to conquer any challenge in front of me. I have to admit that my confidence is sometimes off-putting to people because they interpret it as arrogance. I try to be overt when I'm joking around about something that could be misconstrued as being arrogant, but I am not shy about conveying how confident I am in my abilities. However, I want others to have just as much confidence in themselves as I have in myself.

I was in charge of a funeral procession detail one time, and I had a new officer as part of the assignment. I needed an officer to lead the procession, and the new officer immediately said he couldn't do it because he was new. I could see it on his face and in his body language that he wanted no part of the responsibility of leading the procession. So, naturally, I assigned him to lead the procession. I gave him a quick pep talk, and off we went. He did just fine, and we didn't have any issues. Afterward, I let him know that I had all the confidence in him, but I needed him to have more confidence in himself. That's what I see as our charge as leaders: to help people see that they can achieve more than they believe they can achieve. That's where I get the most joy out of leading people.

When it comes to getting results, I don't rely on luck. Whenever someone has a big moment ahead of them, it's common for people to wish them luck, especially their loved ones or significant other. If I am going into a situation that I have prepared for, an interview, a speech, a test, etc., I don't acknowledge luck. My wife has learned over the years that I will not accept the comment, "Good luck," as she bids me farewell prior to a big moment. Instead, she says, "Do well." That fits more appropriately because it implies that I have everything I need to be successful. I just need to put it all together. Luck is not what I need in those moments; I just need to be the best version of myself. If I have prepared properly, which I feel I do almost always, then I will have success. Now, there are plenty of situations that are out of my control, and in those cases, I want all the "Good lucks" I can muster up.

My wife asked me one time where my confidence came from. I had to really think about it because it wasn't a singular moment. I think it was built over time from being in challenging situations where I learned the most about myself. I learned a lot about life and how your mindset can be your greatest tool to overcome whatever is in your path. So, if you have poured everything that you have within you into preparing for success, you don't have to worry about the outcomes because they are going to be in your favor. That doesn't mean you are going to get every job, promotion, or assignment, but when you know that you gave it everything that you had to give, that is success. If you apply that in your personal and professional life, the results will start to show, and you will see a shift in the outcomes around you. Cooper Kupp was named MVP of Super Bowl LVI. During a post-game interview, he said that he wasn't anxious or nervous about how the game would turn out because he knew he was playing *from* victory, not *for* victory. That type of mindset could be the difference between your dreams only being dreams or turning into reality.

So, if you have poured everything that you have within you into preparing for success, you don't have to worry about the outcomes because they are going to be in your favor.

When I first set out to be a police chief, it was purely about my individual goals and desires. I wanted to be in charge, so I was going to put in the work to ensure I achieved my goals. What I started to recognize before I reached the chief seat was that getting to the seat was going to be the easy part. Navigating the chief seat was going to be a completely different challenge. When you get to the chief seat, you realize that you can no longer make decisions based on your personal outlook. You have to look at what contributes to the greater good, and sometimes, that is someone else getting the credit for what you originally offered up or you taking the blame for someone else's mishap. That's the part of leadership that people don't often realize they are signing up for.

One thing that helps me be at peace with how things unfold is the fact that I have accomplished everything I set out to do in the profession. At the age of 38, I had made it to the chief's seat for the first time. At the age of 39, I was police chief of one of the most known police departments in the world. Accomplishing my goals at such an early age helped me balance things out because I was no longer worried about my achievements anymore. Of course, I wanted to be successful, but my success was now attached to the work of others, not my own. It no longer mattered how many hours I worked into the night or how much I did on the weekends. The only thing that mattered was how my staff showed up for the community, if they understood the mission, and if the community felt safe.

My happiest moments as a chief were when I received an email, or someone came up to me in public to tell me how appreciative they were of one of my officers. Hearing those stories about compassion, patience, or genuine care for what someone was going through—that is what it is all about, and when your community experiences those things from its police officers, things are headed in the right direction.

When I look back over my career, one area in which I feel I have had tremendous results is the media. Early on, I had a desire to be on the news, speaking on behalf of the department. After going to media training, I had a few opportunities to represent the department in the media. As I got further along in my career, I started paying more attention to high-profile incidents from around the country, and I would watch the chief or the sheriff in the press conference and dissect how they answered questions. I would inject myself into their shoes and plan how I would answer questions given the situation that resulted in the need for a press conference in the first place. I learned a lot from doing this; I definitely saw a difference between the leaders who were comfortable up there talking and the ones who were not.

When I went to Ferguson, all of that media training and preparation came full circle because now I was the one in the spotlight. I have definitely had my ups and downs with the media. As my good friend Julie Parker would say, "Run it like a newsroom or get run over!" I have definitely been run over a few times, but overall, I have done well in navigating my relationship with the media. One of the keys to being a public figure with multiple stakeholder groups to connect with is the understanding that your words matter an awful lot.

If my words came across as too supportive of my officers and my department, some people in the community would attack that as not being willing to hold them accountable when the situation warranted accountability. If my words came across as too supportive of community advocates or activists, some of my staff would attack that as not having their back. What I continue to rely on when in the media is speaking with intentionality. Regardless of the topic I'm speaking about, regardless of who may or may not like what I have to say, I want the viewer to feel the intentionality behind my words, whether they agree with them or not.

I still follow critical incidents from around the country and watch how law enforcement leaders navigate the media. When I was the chief in Ferguson, I had to be mindful of the effect of my words at all times. I wasn't just worried about upsetting people; my words could set off protests or civil unrest. This didn't just impact me; protest and unrest were a mental and physical drain on my department and had a significant impact on the community.

While I was a captain in Forest Park, I remember an incident involving our mayor where officers had an interaction with him at his home. The mayor had clearly been under the influence of an intoxicant. He was belligerent and disrespectful toward the officers on scene. More significantly, he had damaged his neighbor's property. The incident was kept quiet around the police department; I didn't even know about it until the media found out about it and came calling. I still remember the interview our department representative did and how damaging it was for some of us within the department. Personally, I didn't feel we handled the incident or the media very well, and it made us look bad. From what I learned of the incident, I felt the mayor received preferential treatment because he was the mayor, which isn't right. Everyone who talked to me about that incident felt as though the mayor got special treatment, and our public explanation of the matter didn't convince anyone otherwise. Bad news doesn't get any better with time.

If you hold true to your values as an organization, you can navigate the media challenges and come out on the other side with your respect and dignity. The incident I shared earlier about the Ferguson officer who was indicted for assault of an arrestee is a prime example of this. That was a horrible incident, but because we were true to our values, we fared well in the media and with the public. We handled the situation the proper way and followed our policies on reporting matters so we did not experience a negative impact.

I make it a point to work with the media to highlight the positive things we are doing within the police department or out in the community so people can see the good side of the department. The birthday parade I spoke of earlier is a great example of that. We received all types of positive news coverage for that event. Having the Ferguson platform helped me get in front of the media quite often, and I leveraged that to expand on the work we were doing.

After George Floyd was killed, I was called to do media interviews for local, national, and international outlets. I took advantage of that to highlight the great work we were doing in Ferguson as a result of our reform efforts. While so much was being talked about the reforms people wanted to see, I had a long list of things we were already doing in Ferguson that could be duplicated across the country. This accomplished two things for me: Ferguson was getting positive news coverage for a change, and media outlets saw that I was willing to speak with them. That led to me receiving more requests to speak on important matters facing law enforcement.

Once I left Ferguson, some of my associates felt I was taking a step back by not taking another high-profile position. I have been pleased to see that my media presence has largely remained intact. *Good Morning America 3* did the story on our children's book in Apex, and *ABC News* continues to bring me in to speak on high-profile incidents that impact the country. Having a law enforcement presence in the national media is key for us to continue to add our voices to the topics that impact the country. If we are not active with the media, then everyone else is speaking on our behalf, and they don't have the experience or the expertise to do it like we can.

Working with the media can be very intimidating. When I talk to some of my colleagues around the country about the media, they often express their hatred for them. They often feel that the media intentionally tries to display law enforcement in a negative light. One of my first media interviews in Ferguson was done by a reporter with whom I would never talk to again. This reporter, who worked for a nationally recognized newspaper, wrote an article that was intended to be divisive and invoke animosity toward the department.

While there are a handful of reporters or outlets that thrive on negativity, I feel the majority of media professionals are not intentionally out to "get us." There are times when we can use the media to get what we want. As the chief in Apex, my community suffered a horrible tragedy when two of our residents were shot and killed by a neighbor. Apex had never seen anything like this before, and it was tragic all the way around. When something like this happens, the media requests start flooding in immediately.

One of the top requests is for 911 calls because they are usually public records. In this instance, one of the 911 calls was from one of the victims, and it was extremely difficult to listen to. Our legal team confirmed that we had to release that call along with the other ones, but I did not want the public to be traumatized by the call, and I didn't want the families of the victims to have to relive their nightmares by hearing them, either. I held a press conference prior to releasing the calls, during which I explained what was on them. I read a statement from both families and then implored the media outlets not to play the one call from the victim. It worked! No one played that audio clip, and I was appreciative that the families didn't have to experience that.

The last thing I want to highlight about the media and how to leverage working with them is to understand your community and how they receive information. In all my years, I have never seen anything quite like The Real STL News, an online (Facebook) media outlet in the St. Louis area. As I mentioned earlier in the book, I learned of my confirmation in Ferguson while watching a live stream from them. Essentially, they were a group of individuals who all had access to the Facebook page, and whoever was closest would show up and go live from the scene of whatever was going on. I'm not sure how many of them were on the team, but it felt like hundreds because they would be everywhere.

The Real STL News has an enormous following, and I used their page often to gauge how the community was feeling about things going on in Ferguson or related to law enforcement. They covered a lot in Ferguson, especially our protest and civil unrest events. Knowing that I needed to connect to their audience, if I saw them show up at a scene and I had an update to give, I would go over and do a live interview with them.

Working with some other community leaders, we conducted a live-streamed sit-down between law enforcement, community resource leaders, and community youths to hear what the youths needed from the adults in the community to better help them succeed. I will never forget receiving an email from TMZ about a video that had gone public of a police officer hitting a fleeing suspect with their vehicle. TMZ was trying to confirm which jurisdiction the officer worked for—which wasn't Ferguson, by the way—before they shared the story, but that story broke first on The Real STL News. Being willing to connect with the community in out-of-the-box ways has definitely contributed to me seeing positive results in the various communities in which I have served.

The thing I'm most proud of about my career is the contribution I've made to helping people understand or learn something they were previously oblivious to. These are sometimes difficult conversations to have with people, but they are so rewarding if you have a breakthrough. I was reviewing a use-of-force incident one time and listening to the audio from the body microphone the officer was wearing. The officer did not have a body camera, but the patrol car he was driving had a dash camera, so the mic was synced up with the dash camera.

The suspect fled on foot, and the officer chased after him. While I couldn't see what happened once the officer caught the suspect, I could hear what was going on. As the officer chased the suspect, he yelled either, "Boy, stop running!" or "Stop running, boy!" I can't remember the exact order of his words. He eventually tackled the suspect and took him into custody. There was no problem with the level or amount of force used; everything was done according to policy. But I had a problem with the "boy" comment, so I called him in to talk to him about it.

I simply asked him why he'd called the suspect "boy," and the officer explained that it was because he was a juvenile. The suspect was, in fact, a child. I don't recall his exact age, but he was around 15 or 16 years old. I was hoping that was the explanation the officer was going to give me. Next, I asked the officer if he was familiar with the racial undertone of a white male calling a black male "boy." He was not familiar with this, so I went on to explain how, historically, the term "boy" was used in a derogatory way to display dominance and authority over black males. I explained that although he was chasing someone who was a juvenile, it still was in his best interest not to use that word because he could find himself in a situation where someone looked young but was actually of adult age, and they might take serious offense. The young officer was very appreciative of the information I shared and understood how that could put him in a dangerous situation if someone felt disrespected and, instead of running from him, decided they now wanted to confront and possibly assault him.

I had an officer who worked for me in Ferguson who was strong-willed and highly opinionated on matters. We butted heads on several matters during my time there, but overall, I appreciated the energy this officer brought to the department. If we were headed into battle, this was definitely an officer that I wanted by my side. This officer worked in a specialty position and had created a challenge coin with his own money for his specialty position. If you know anything about challenge coins, you know how these things are extremely coveted in law enforcement. The officer was selling these coins to raise money for the specialty team. I haven't read about the specific origin of challenge coins, but what I do know is that these coins are typically earned by the people who receive them.

One day, I was walking through the hallway of the PD, and I ran into this officer as he was showing off this new challenge coin. First, he explains how he'd designed it to ensure he did not violate any of our department's policies. When you're the chief, "I didn't break any rules" is typically the first explanation you get about anything. After seeing the coin, I asked him if he was giving it to me. I can't share exactly what he said in this book, but he used some colorful language to say no. He told me I could buy one if I wanted to get one. I turned down his offer to purchase one, and we both went on with our day.

Fast-forward some months later, and we were in the middle of the civil unrest stemming from George Floyd's death. After the violence we experienced early on had subsided, we had to deal with regular protests every evening, not knowing if further violence was waiting for us. One night, a group of protestors began marching down the middle of the roadway. We were not set up for marches through town, so my officers had to get in front of this group and get them to move the march to the sidewalk. This officer was the one who had to engage with the protestors to get their cooperation. The interaction ended with him and the protest leaders shaking hands, and the group moved out of the road. MSNBC reporters captured the encounter, and they aired the footage the next day.

It was a great example of how things had changed in our response to protests since the 2014 civil unrest erupted.

When I did an on-air interview with MSNBC the next day, I was able to highlight the good work my officers were doing despite the violence and destruction we had suffered just days earlier. As we were briefing for that night's protest, I gave the officer a shoutout in front of his peers and highlighted to the group that we could still come and get the job done with compassion and professionalism. The more we highlighted that for the community and world to see, the more benefits we would reap from it on the backend of the chaos. The next day, without me asking, that officer handed me one of his challenge coins. Nothing needed to be said; it was a sign of appreciation. I had earned the coin, and that was one of the few bright moments in my life during that time.

We have all heard the phrases "Leadership is lonely" or "Life is lonely at the top." We hear it so often because it's true. My journey has been no different. I am a firm believer that you have to be the leader that is needed, not the leader that is wanted. I have found that people are often more inclined to speak up about what they want versus what they need. As the leader, you have to be able to look out across the entire landscape of the organization or group you lead and discern what is needed. You are not able to explain everything to everyone with the level of detail you would like. You sometimes receive information that is not conducive to being disseminated in a timely manner, if at all.

Breaking it down to its simplest form, being a leader is about getting positive results. We forget how important the word positive is when we talk about reform, results, or change. All outcomes are not positive, and if you label yourself an agent of change, hopefully, you are not leading negative change because that is still change. Results boil down to making decisions, and as a leader, you can not shy away from that task. For me, that is the only thing that separates a quality leader from someone I would not feel comfortable following.

I don't mind when a wrong decision is made. I don't advocate for wrong decisions, but decisions have to be made, and as the leader, that falls to you. I have made some good decisions, and I have made some bad ones. I have done the right thing in moments, and I have done the wrong thing in moments. Regardless of the outcome of the decision, charge forward because another decision moment is waiting for you. Trust what you have poured into yourself. Trust that you have prepared for the moment because most of us have. If leadership were for everyone, then we wouldn't need leaders. Know that you belong and that you bring tremendous value to the seat you sit in.

Another phrase that I use often is "Life comes for all of us." It doesn't matter who you are. It does not matter what town you grew up in. It does not matter what neighborhood you live in or how much money you have in your bank account. We all have to deal with the trials and tribulations of life. If we treat one another like we're all dealing with those trials and tribulations, maybe we wouldn't be so mean to one another. Maybe we wouldn't be so harsh to one another. Maybe we would be more open to giving people the benefit of the doubt. It doesn't mean that we don't address the things that we need to address, but often, there is a sensitive way to address matters. I implore you all to think about that when you're dealing with people, especially the people you lead.

As I begin to wrap things up, there is one result that I never had an opportunity to bring to fruition. I will share it with you all, and the only thing I ask in return is that if you do this, you give me credit for the idea. Deal? Okay, here you go. Since the death of Michael Brown and others across the country, law enforcement has seen its fair share of scrutiny and ridicule. One way this has shown up is in employees in the service industry refusing to serve officers in uniform. We have seen this unfortunate trend in multiple spaces but in restaurants in particular.

When this happens, the response is pretty consistent. The agency the officer works for condemns the establishment for the treatment of the officer, and rightfully so. This is normally followed by a call to action for all law enforcement to boycott the establishment, which is then often followed by a public apology from the establishment for the discriminatory treatment of the officer.

If I were met with such discrimination at a service establishment, my response would be different. Instead of going on a rampage to publicly shame the establishment for employing individuals who would disrespect law enforcement in this manner, I would pull out my phone and record a video while at the business. In the video, I would explain the treatment I just received and share the name of the employee who refused to serve me. I would then encourage all law enforcement in the area to patronize the establishment and ask for the person who refused to serve me.

Here's my rationale for responding in this way. Clearly, this person has not seen enough positive examples of law enforcement in their lives for them to treat me this way. I don't want to discourage them from having a positive interaction with law enforcement. I want to encourage it so they can see that their negative thoughts and feelings shouldn't be directed to everyone in a police uniform. If we have never met before, why would you hate me? Instead of fighting hate with hate, which hasn't gotten us anywhere, why don't we start fighting hate with love? Fortunately, I have not been discriminated against in that way, but if you find yourself in this situation, try my idea and see how positive the outcome will be for you, the person who denied you, and the community at large.

As you all are already aware, you are reading the last chapter of the book. This book has eight chapters for a very intentional reason. I've stated throughout the book that I lead with intentionality. If any of you are familiar with track and field, track events often have runners in eight lanes, and that is the foundation for my connection with the number eight—lane eight, to be specific. I have never been a track and field athlete a day in my life, so the significance of this is not from personal track experience but from witnessing a great feat.

In 2016, I had the amazing opportunity to go to Rio for the Olympics. I was there solely as a spectator. Going to the events in person gave me a different perspective on the games. I definitely paid more attention to those Olympic games than I had previously. One race that I watched was the men's 400-meter sprint final. That was when I learned how the runners are positioned in the lanes. There were eight lanes, and for some of the races, they have to factor in the curves of the track, so they start the runners at different points. That is to account for the distance when you add in the turns; with the stagger, everyone is running the same distance. For this race, lane eight was the most outside lane, which means the runner has to go further on the curves. Because of this, they start in front of everyone else.

What I learned after this race was that they typically put the favorites or the best runners in the middle lanes—three, four, five, and six—so they can pace themselves against one another and have the best finish possible. Consequently, it's fair to say that the runner in the outer lane is not typically expected to be in serious contention to finish near the top, let alone win the race. The biggest disadvantage in running in lane eight is that you have no idea how you're doing in the race. You can't see any of the other runners unless one of them passes you, at which point you know you are not doing that well.

Running in lane eight for this medal race was South Africa's Wade Van Niekerk. The commentators were not talking about him being a contender for the gold medal in the pre-race discussion. The race started, and Van Niekerk was out front because he was in lane eight. As he came around the last turn, he was still out front, and none of the other runners were close to him. Niekerk not only went on to win the gold medal, but he shattered the world record time for the 400 meters. It was an amazing feat, and the commentators couldn't stop talking about how improbable it was for him to not only win the race but to win it from lane eight.

As they marveled at his accomplishment, one of the commentators mentioned that to win this race from lane eight, you essentially have to run for your life. You are running blind and scared! You don't know if someone is going to catch you, so you give maximum effort until the race is over. Listening to the explanation of what it took to win this race from lane eight, I realized that I had been and would continue to approach my career that way. I was running scared, fearful that someone was going to catch me, so I gave maximum effort the entire time. I was running for my life!

At the beginning of this chapter, I talked about confidence and how I built up the ultimate confidence over time. I realized that I built up that confidence because of how I've been running my race. I can't see anybody else in my peripheral vision, and I'm running scared. I'm running like crazy to make sure that I win the race. I haven't broken any world records, but I have broken many glass ceilings along the way. That's the same level of confidence that I want everybody to have in whatever it is that they are doing.

When you're running your race or trying to accomplish something, whatever it is, if you solely focus on what you are pouring into yourself, the results will take care of themselves. Van Niekerk had nothing else to worry about but himself. That was the only thing that he could control; he couldn't see anything else, and he couldn't pull any motivation from anywhere else. You have the power to run your race; you have the power to effect positive change. Therefore, you have the power to be the change. Run scared, run for your life, run knowing that you are running for a purpose that is greater than you. You may not personally reap the benefits of the work you do, but your job in leadership is to leave the space better than how you found it.

When your time is up and you say, "I'm Done Here!" What will you see when you look back on your time in the seat? Have you left the team/group/organization/business/agency in a better place? Did you lay a foundation for sustainable positive impact? Will things be easier for the people who sit in the seat after you because of the sacrifices that you made? The answers to those questions are what defines the impact that you have had. Be intentional to ensure you use your gifts for good in the world. There is no greater feeling than leaving a legacy that your family and friends can be proud of.

I have been blessed beyond measure to have had the career that I've had. It has come with great sacrifice, but I am happy with the results. Here's to running the next phase of your journey with a "lane eight" mentality.

CONCLUSION

When I started my career, I had no idea it would turn out the way it did. I attribute my success to being intentional and authentic in how I approach the challenges of the profession. No matter what community you desire to impact, you have the power to contribute to positive change. First, you have to believe that it is possible. Then, you have to build the confidence that you are the person to get it done. Last, know that you will be successful because of the investment you will make in yourself to make it happen.

There was nothing special about me that contributed to my success. I just put in the work to be great, and that is all that you have to do. One thing you have to remember is that you may not be around to see the fruits of your labor. I remember getting a text message from a former colleague of mine in Ferguson after I had been gone for a couple of years. My former colleague explained that I had popped up in their mind because the town had just approved the installation of a fence at the police department. My former colleague remembered the battles I'd had with leadership years earlier, fighting for that to be done.

I had fought for a fence so officers wouldn't have to stand out on the line for every protest and take verbal abuse from angry protestors. Year after year of that treatment was not healthy for them, and I wanted it to stop.

Although the fence wasn't built during my tenure, I still felt a sense of accomplishment because I knew that my battles had laid the foundation for it. When you lead with intentionality, you focus on the work and the impact. If someone else gets the credit and the benefit, that's okay. Your sacrifice was worth it.

Thank you for going on this journey with me to a better understanding of how to deal with conflict, challenges, and obstacles in your professional life. As I lived out my story, it never felt noteworthy or more important than anyone else's. It was only when I began traveling the country, sharing tidbits of my story, that I started to understand that I had something special to share.

I hope you have found my story enlightening and entertaining. Every one of us can do remarkable things. No matter where you are in life, you have a value that no one else possesses. My hope for everyone who has just finished reading this book is that you have a greater sense of responsibility to impact change in the space you are in. No profession is perfect; they all have room for improvement. Know that you are special and equipped to drive positive change.

Know that you have value and that everyone you encounter has value. The sky *is* the limit when you invest in your *why*. If you truly have prepared yourself to take on the burden of leadership, then bask in the possibilities. I was a dreamer, and all of my dreams have come true. That is the power of belief in one's self. Are you willing to dream for the future you want? Can you envision dreaming so big that when you tell people about your plans for your future, they think it's comical?

I remember telling a friend of mine about my plans to become a police chief, and he laughed at them. He did not see me as a chief, and that was okay. That same friend commented on a social media post of mine after I was a chief and referenced our conversation about my dreams and desire to be a chief. People don't have to believe in your dreams, but you do.

Know that you belong and hold tremendous value. It may require you to take on the toughest challenge in your country, but guess what? You're built to handle it!

When I was a captain in Forest Park, I reached a point where I felt ready to become a police chief. Although no opportunities were in sight, I was confident that I would become a chief in the not-too-distant future. Anyone who knows me well knows I'm a sucker for a good deal. One day, I received an email about Nike polo shirts on sale, with free embroidery included. When considering what to have embroidered, I decided on "Chief Armstrong." I didn't know how long it would take before I could actually wear those shirts, but I wanted the motivation of seeing them in my closet every day, reminding me of what I was working toward. I couldn't slack off—I had to keep grinding because I didn't want to waste money on shirts I couldn't wear. It turns out that one of my most iconic photos is from an impromptu press conference the morning after intense rioting in Ferguson. You'll recognize it if you see it—I'm wearing one of my 'Chief Armstrong' Nike polos.

I have run my race and accomplished my goals. Now I help others impact their world as I have impacted mine. I consult with and coach leaders to help them navigate the challenges of leadership. I travel the globe, giving training courses and dialogues that challenge people to strive for greater heights in the work that they do. I'm committed to inspiring the next generation of impactful leaders through a catalog of topics that are sure to ignite action. You can find more information about the work I do and connect with me on my website: jasonparmstrong.com. Let's get to work and impact change together!

THANK YOU FOR READING MY BOOK!

Just to say thanks for buying and reading my book, I would like to give you a free welcome call with me!

Scan the QR Code:

I appreciate your interest in my book and value your feedback as it helps me improve future versions of this book. I would appreciate it if you could leave your invaluable review on Amazon.com with your feedback. Thank you!

Made in the USA
Columbia, SC
28 October 2024

16450a66-f3d2-4d60-84e5-771d8f3a2474R01